THE LIFESTYLE ENTREPRENEUR

HOW TO TURN YOUR INTERESTS INTO MONEY

CATO HOEBEN
ANGELA NEUSTATTER

GIBSON SQUARE

www.lifestyle-entrepreneur.net

658·1141

First published by Gibson Square

Available as an e-book

info@gibsonsquare.com
www.gibsonsquare.com
Tel: +44 (0)20 7096 1100 (UK)
Tel: +1 646 216 9813 (USA)

ISBN 978-1-78334-001-9

CONTENTS

Foreword   5
Introduction: What is a Lifestyle Entrepreneur   9

Why Become a Lifestyle Entrepreneur   13
Do I Have What It Takes?   24
We All Have Skills: Identify Yours   37
Your Innerpreneur   58
Can I Learn to Be an Entrepreneur   73
The Business of Funding   83
Tech Savviness   104
Getting Going   122
Keeping Going   135
The Money Stuff   153
The Integrated Life   161
What Success Looks Like   173
The 5-Step Plan   183

Acknowledgements   190
Resources   191

I dedicate this book to Carolina, my beautiful wife who has supported me through tough times writing this book and beyond, my father Olly, the first Lifestyle Entrepreneur I came across in my life and a great role model and, of course, my inspiring co-author and mother who has been a huge help in pulling everything together.

AUTHORS' NOTE

This book is written by both Cato Hoeben and Angela Neustatter, but where the word 'I' is used it refers to Cato as the book is based on his experiences as a Lifestyle Entrepreneur.

FOREWORD

Imagine you had free reign to explore your passions, hobbies and interests no matter what they were. Shaping the day around what you love doing, enjoying a lifestyle that suits you according to your schedule, one that fits around how *you* work rather than that of an employer. Or maybe just imagine being able to free up time to spend with your family and friends or choose when you want to take holidays at a moment's notice.

Four years ago, I would have told you that kind of Utopian set-up doesn't exist. I would have laughed at the idea of creating my own timetable and earning money from my passion, mainly because everyone (and everything around me) didn't work that way. A lifestyle like that seemed way too perfect and the level of freedom and financial stability would be unsustainable. Or so I thought.

I was travelling regularly to Spain to be with my Spanish girlfriend, but I was stressed. In order to earn money to live on I was going back to London every two weeks for a part-time job with a mental health charity as a web editor and I was exhausted all the time. Though cheaper than travel within the UK, the flights were expensive, as was life in London during my stays there.

I seemed to spend way too much time rushing to catch the bus and worrying about getting late to the airport, and about the colossal amount of work I had to do which mounted up because of the amount of time wasted in transit. I was concerned about earning enough to pay the bills. Compounding my stress was the fact that in Spain, where I wanted to be with my girlfriend, unemployment rates had reached alarmingly high levels (just under 26% in 2015 according to Reuters) so the chances of getting a job there were zilch.

What I didn't realise then was that a silent work revolution was taking place around me. Whereas I was used to assuming that companies essentially had a monopoly on offering employment, the Internet was eroding this monopoly at an increasingly rapid pace. Websites were creating an increasing number of different platforms that brought together buyers and sellers of a huge variety/range of products and services. The revolutionary consumer motto of eBay, Amazon and other marketplaces that anyone should be able to get anything from anywhere was now being applied to the working world.

Ebay, in a way, has always offered everyone a new job. We all know the stories of people who are making a very good living out of setting up shop on Ebay and selling products more cheaply than elsewhere, or flogging other people's unwanted stuff. But now there were websites bringing together people for very specific products and services.

Anything is possible, from selling eBooks (by the author themselves), email marketing services, online and offline courses on websites that connect teachers and learners and selling mobile apps to offering things like bookkeeping and design services. Those who decide to offer such services are visible to anyone in the world as well as the people they happen to know.

The web has also been changing the direct link between work and remuneration. There are, for example, free make-up blogs and other websites that are so successful that advertisers pay to have their products linked to them. They create an income stream for the people who run them that doesn't come directly from the people who use the site or users.

It was when I realised that for my set up to work, I had to find a way to increase my salary that I started to look for alternatives. I was extremely unlikely to be able to have a more senior role or earn more in my part-time job which left me broke every month because of the cost of commuting to Spain. Getting promoted would almost certainly depend on being more visible in the office, which meant not being in Spain so often, while the increase in responsibilities would mean even more stress if I did continue trying to keep my long-distance relationship in Spain alive (which mattered to me a great deal).

I was already physically exhausted by everything I had to do. I was feeling very unhealthy and something had to give. I began investigating different ways to earn a living.

I looked at becoming a freelancer, but quickly realised that I would be even worse off than in my job. In addition, I would have none of the security I had in my job at the charity. As a freelancer, you often follow the employer-employee model even though you are purely hired to do a job. And you are often even more dependent than in a regular job, because without warning your stream of work may come to an end. You have to make sure that your employer really likes working with you, because if they don't, too often there are 10 other freelancers who can do the same job as well as you.

It was then that, quite by chance, I made my first step as a Lifestyle Entrepreneur.

INTRODUCTION

What Is a Lifestyle Entrepreneur?

I had always been passionate about music. But I had been told repeatedly by friends, relatives and people in the industry that it's near-impossible to make money from music unless you're incredibly famous or win Britain's Got Talent. The frustrating thing is that, as in many industries, there *is* money in music, but it often has to trickle through various sets of hands before it reaches you. By that point you're looking at being able to purchase a couple of Curly Wurlys or half a Mars Bar with your earnings.

But as I was desperate to find a way to earn a living that did not involve commuting and could be home-based, I started looking at music again. I didn't have much to lose. To my surprise there were a number of options that I hadn't thought about before. I'd come across earning via things like affiliate schemes where you sell other people's products as that's a common way to earn online. But a lot of these ideas were new to me, such as selling stock music via online marketplaces for the general public to use in their own multimedia projects.

The impression I'd had was that it's prohibitively expensive and complicated to do something like that. But the more I searched, the more I came across people who were earning well from their music and other skills. More importantly, they seemed to be so much happier than I was.

I decided to open a few accounts on the various websites I came across that allowed me to sell my music online, as I wanted to test the waters and see the reaction my music would get. It took me no more than a few hours. Quite quickly, I started getting some sales on the sites I'd uploaded to. I didn't know these people personally at all, nor did they know me. But that didn't matter to any of us, nor where we lived. All that mattered was that they needed music for a specific purpose right now, were willing to pay for it, and I was able to provide it to them there and then.

Instead of time-consuming pitches, phone calls, and follow-up emails that went on forever, these transactions took seconds. Admittedly, the money wasn't much to write home about. But I had merely put together *what I thought* would sell and uploaded it. I had spent almost no time on it, with no market research, no analysis of what was in demand, nor a business plan. I had just dipped a toe in it, and it felt good.

I then looked at my competitors, and evaluated what I needed to do in order to stand out and attract more clients. The market was filled with very talented people, but I could also see that even composers with music more poorly produced and structured than mine were still earning more, so I started uploading music regularly. During the weeks that followed, I began getting a number of sales, particularly from a site called AudioJungle, which is part of a popular network of sites run by envato.com/sites. On these sites you can sell not only music, but a range of stock media, from photos, videos, and design assets like illustrations, to website themes and even 3D models that animators can use in their projects.

It was an amazing feeling, turning what I'd been told for so many years on its head. My music was in demand. The thing I most loved doing was making me money. As in many industries, it was easy to see who I was competing against and what was in demand on sites like AudioJungle because they displayed things like bestseller lists very much like the ones you see on Amazon. I got a clear sense of the quality and type of music for which there was a lively demand. Already after the first month it was clear I could earn regularly from my music. But it was also clear that I would need to continue working in other areas in order to sustain this type of lifestyle. I decided to continue building websites while building up other streams of income, music being the primary one.

As I made my way in this Lifestyle Entrepreneur world, I saw how it's a way that an increasing number of mid-lifers and those around retirement age are choosing. It makes sense when you hear about someone like Matt Stone, who had a successful career in car sales but felt as he matured that the company treated him with less respect. He cut loose and set up a number of small projects which now bring an income and give him personal satisfaction. Tim Hulse, 54, who was unceremoniously laid off by the company he had worked with for years, pitched into despair for a while. But then he realised he could re-create his life so that he continued working and doing something that met his wish of being 'meaningful'. He started EcoVert Solutions, a sustainable construction company. And I could name plenty more start-up entrepreneurs nearer my parents' generations than my own.

I then took my own second step as a Lifestyle Entrepreneur. On the sites I had found, I wasn't restricted to just music. I could sell a website design, HTML newsletter templates, voice-over work, become a virtual assistant, translate texts from Spanish to English, and even offer sound design for companies that needed audio to accompany the intro of their corporate videos. I was starting to see a way out of my stressful 9-8 job that was slowly killing me.

So I reckoned, what if I combined a number of different skills I had and made them available on these websites, packaged in a similar way to how I was making my music available? If I could create a basket of several earning streams, then I could potentially make the same as, or more than, what I was making now. Yes, it meant I needed to start thinking about work in a different way from my regular job, but I wasn't exactly complaining. I was finally seeing how I could escape from the corner I seemed to have painted myself into.

As I'd worked for a media company that specialises in websites and digital marketing, I'd picked up a few tricks on how to build sites. I'd learnt how to write appealing marketing copy, research well, and produce educational videos about science while working there. My background in music also meant selling other audio-related services could be an option.

Not forgetting my education, I had also done a Masters in Science Communication which had provided me with a range of useful skills ranging from journalism, narrative development and dissecting complex scientific papers into an understandable form, to something as arcane as semiotic analysis. During that time, I had also learnt about documentary film-making, interview techniques, and even something as wide-ranging as project management, an essential skill used in every industry and not just media or music. Finally there was website coding, writing reports and data entry.

All of those skills are useful in a business context. Businesses expect to pay for such services and therefore these skills provided me with a bunch of potential revenue streams. It got me thinking about how else I might expand my potential earnings to be able to sustain myself. I urgently needed a plan.

This book will tell you what I did next, and how I became a full-blown Lifestyle Entrepreneur. I'm now able to be in Spain or London as much as I want and whenever I want, have married my girlfriend and am far happier and at peace with myself than I've ever been. I wrote this book so that others can also become a Lifestyle Entrepreneur and, in fact, wish I had read this book four years ago, as it took me that long to muddle through the principles of what I was doing and how I could surf the demand for my services and remain financially afloat.

You will find not only me as an example, but also others who have become successful Lifestyle Entrepreneurs. Some have wanted to gain as much business success as possible, others have significantly increased their spare time to be with their family, while others have maximised other things they value in their life such as ecology or social work.

The one thing they all have in common is that they are bosses of their own destiny, whether one-man or larger, and shape their livelihoods to their own tune, not that of others. What *they* find important, they set out to achieve. It is the world we live in today that is creating these possibilities and I hope this book will inspire you to believe that there is a Lifestyle Entrepreneur in every one of us.

1

WHY BECOME A LIFESTYLE ENTREPRENEUR?

If there is an answer the question, 'why become a Lifestyle Entrepreneur?' in a single sentence, it would be a way of living where you earn from the things you're passionate about, where both work and free time are enjoyable. As an LE you direct your energies towards incorporating your individual skills, interests and passions into ways of working. The daily routine and structure within your life feeds back to you not just financially, but in terms of choosing how much free time you will take, being excited about having control over how much work you can get done, and finding ways of supporting yourself that are genuinely rewarding.

As an LE you may well work as hard as, or harder than, in a 9 - 5 job, as people who take on this lifestyle after they have worked in a conventional job will know, but you do it on your terms. You do not sell your time to somebody else to decide how it must be used. You are in control of deciding how you work, how best to use your talents and creativity to design a lifestyle that suits you.

Ever since I quit a traditional full-time job to set up my own work streams, I feel I have flexed my creative and entrepreneurial muscles and seen how working my way even through the hard times is far more rewarding than climbing a career ladder for someone else's business.

Multi-stream earning
An integral part of what I define as being a Lifestyle Entrepreneur is creating multiple ways to earn an income, as I have done over

the four years since I decided to take on this lifestyle. So, you might have one job that will bring in a small amount of money, like my music did in the beginning, but combining lots of these small sources of income can create a decent salary. Or perhaps smaller streams can grow into bigger, more significant streams, as has been the case with my music.

In the beginning, the web development work I was doing brought in far more money but, because that's not what I most enjoy doing, I am taking on less and earning less in order to have time for my music which I am building as an income stream. However, the voice-overs I began doing a few months ago as well have built steadily, compensating for the loss, and I enjoy doing them more. Perhaps it sounds a little 'dilettantish', but if you persevere and make this way work it is empowering, and there is a real thrill in thinking that you might hit on a hobby you have always enjoyed. With a little time spent working out how you might market it, that hobby can become a way of earning.

I, and other Lifestyle Entrepreneurs, call this 'multi-stream earning' and the very real advantage of this is that, by going it alone, you are not relying on a single line of work. Here too, older LEs may benefit from skills learned in how the world of work and the marketplace function.

With the type of work where you are dependent on others for whether the business lives or dies, you can feel little control over if and when you will suddenly be left high, dry and broke. Or, as I have seen happening, you are suddenly made redundant by a firm, or a decent contract is replaced with one which, in terms of security, is virtually worthless. Perhaps you find there are no other jobs or, if any of the other harsh hazards of today's workplace hit you, you might find you are dependent on others for your economic survival. You can be left feeling hopeless, helpless and shoved back into the pecking line of passing CVs around to prospective employers. Being responsible for your own destiny, for firing yourself (or your clients) if a line of work really isn't paying off does not leave you feeling impotent in the way that being told you don't have a job any more, or your pay is being cut, does.

Of course, it can be hard and there is nobody to say: 'you've done a day's work, go home and rest'. Sometimes, I may tear my hair juggling three or four very different tasks, but I have learned to cope with that because it is *my choice*. If I am overloaded one day, I can always decide to adjust the hours I will work the next day or so by setting the alarm to times during which I work best. As long as I meet my deadline and the work is good enough, everyone is happy. That may not be so easy in the average workplace.

I love the fact that I have, at present, three very different sources of income: music, voice-overs, and web design. It means I might be working on a website for an artist (Tracey Emin) in the morning, composing music for a film in the afternoon and then, just as I am signing off, an email arrives asking me to do the voice-over for an advert and it is no sweat to take another half hour or so of what was planned as free time to do it as I enjoy it. I know I can do it well using my own judgement, not that of a boss.

Beating the insecure workplace

I know how scary it can feel to hear endless stories of a contracting workplace and I have seen how grim it is for young people who want to work who have studied, done apprenticeships, NVQs, diplomas, degrees and so on. People who have worked hard for qualifications they believed would take them into employment, but find there is nothing for them.

According to 2015 government figures, young people are nearly three times more likely to be unemployed than the rest of the population, the largest gap in more than 20 years. The number of people aged 16-24 who are not in full-time education or employment has increased by 8,000 over the last quarter according to a report by the House of Commons library for Labour published in 2015. One outcome may be that those who see no prospect of employment become disillusioned and possibly depressed.

But the flip side of this is that ageism is alive and well in employers' minds according to Emma Jacobs in the *Financial Times*.

As she points out, 'some employers characterise workers even in their fifties, let alone their sixties, as expensive, inflexible, out of touch, technologically illiterate and coasting to retirement' (*Working older*, FT Magazine, July 3rd 2013).

So how valuable it is to see a different way. To find, as I have researching this book, the number of people discovering their inner entrepreneur, to create work for themselves and realise they can sell their skills. In some cases, they are building up successful businesses and can side step the all-or-nothing mantra that so many of us have grown up with. A mantra that considers you a 'failure' or 'doomed' to a second-rate life if you do not get the credentials to be employed in a marketplace like everyone else. A marketplace where, with the scarcity and fragility of stable employment these days, employers rule.

The sociologist Zygmunt Bauman talked of liquid modernity to describe a situation where the expectation of security is an illusion, and I would say that goes for all age groups in a work environment that is insecure and ever shifting, and I have spoken to a number of people who see LE as a way of combatting being at the mercy of this illusion. I count myself among them.

Democratic

The Lifestyle Entrepreneur way is also democratic, in the way Karl Marx saw workers' controlling the means of production as being, while the increasingly top down workplace so often is not. Your education, ethnicity, socio-economic background or which school you went to are nobody's business. If you have the ability to train up in a skill, however basic, quirky, geeky, intellectually off the wall, financially astute or socially valuable, then you have the potential to be a multi-stream earner.

Choosing the Lifestyle Entrepreneur route may mean you have to go on working in a conventional job or part-time job to support yourself while you build the LE businesses, as we see some of the people interviewed are doing.

But if you have psychologically distanced yourself from the

idea that pleasing the-powers-that-be in the workplace is where all your creative energy must go, you can experiment, you can try things out, you can ask yourself some important questions:

'Okay, do I like doing what I've studied for the last 15 years of my life? Do I really enjoy and want to make money from it? Is it giving me any kind of soul satisfaction and am I actually contributing something that I think will be useful in the future? Am I creating a community around me that I am happy with?'

I believe that for a lot of people at work, none of this is the case. I know banker friends of mine and, from what I can see and what they tell me, they are not particularly connected with the community around them. They often strike me as very isolated. Combined with the hard-nosed business approach of that industry, which is mainly about making lots of money, that way of living doesn't strike me as particularly conducive to a happy existence. In contrast, the LE style of living allows you to create a community in which you can actually be well supported and feel like you are a part of something.

In many ways, today's younger generations have been fed a fat lie. They've been told that if you work hard at your studies, give up all notion of a free-range childhood with time to find out what delights you and experiment with different hobbies and activities, and instead just buckle down to piles of homework to get top marks, then you can put yourself on the road to wealth and status.

As so many high-performing graduates have found, never mind those with less glowing credentials but bags of enthusiasm and creativity, the workplace is not a place for them. And if work is offered, the chances of it being the kind of secure, pension-backed job for life, which was at least the notion of how work should be for earlier generations, are virtually zilch. Forget caring paternalism and think zero-hour contracts.

Older generations may not feel so acutely let down as the workplace has, on the whole, offered opportunities and the impression of security. But in 2011, five percent of under 30-year-olds - which given today's longevity projections is still young - were made redundant. In 2007, it was recorded that a third of men aged 55-64 and women aged 55-59 were unemployed, inactive or retired according to Alison Maitland in her report for the Equal Opportunities Commission (2010) *Working Better - Over 50s, The New Work Generation.*

Older workers are finding it harder than any other age group to get back into work after being made redundant in the recession says Alison Maitland. So increasingly, sustaining a career until 70 will become a pressing issue says Jacobs. Might these become the new 'olderpreneurs'?

So thinking outside the box and finding the inner entrepreneur in the workplace is very important as we mature. It is inspiring to come across people like Suzanne Noble, in her 50s, a powerhouse of ideas and determination who continues to experiment and push forward with new ideas and businesses. She has to spread two hands of fingers wide to count the number of start-ups she has been responsible for, and we will hear more of her in due course.

So if we are getting profound, I believe this way of working has the potential to undermine the iron grip of the hierarchical workplace, what it offers and what it can demand. It presents a far more democratic way for us to offer ourselves a different way of feeling about a life in which we must work to live.

Challenge and contact

Having a range of different jobs is stimulating, challenging, and keeps you in touch with a far wider range of people than is often the case in, say, an office job. Nor do you have a single person planning the way you should work and benefiting from the profits you make.

But I hadn't worked any of this out when I jumped ship from my job with a new media production company in London. I hadn't realised that, although I had studied towards this career, the business of spending five days a week in an office 9am-8pm would leave me stressed and frustrated. I couldn't do the work the way I felt was best and had to accept the creative judgement of a boss I did not think was getting it right much of the time. Perhaps I was just a bolshy upstart, but whatever it was, I began to feel my health was suffering. I had a girlfriend living in Spain, but too little time and too few emotional resources to give the relationship, which I very much wanted to work, a fair chance.

Feeling trapped

When I sat down and made a list of the reasons I felt I had to find a way to change the situation, this is what I came up with:

- Spending time with my family.
- Being more productive, as I often felt I was wasting time at the office when there was nothing to do or, conversely, overworked and ending up so fatigued I wasn't producing my best work.
- Contributing something useful or creative to the world (music in my case).
- Freeing up time to do more sport.
- Earning more money in a smarter way (the 'work smarter, not harder' mentality).
- Avoiding the commute.

That list was a wake up call. I wasn't happy, I was doing work that wasn't what I had envisaged during my studies, and I didn't see it ever really calling on my creative side. I knew I felt trapped, but had no idea what else I could I do. At that point I began to look around and see that people were working for themselves, making a living and having a life that seemed to bring private and work life together quite harmoniously. I wanted to be one of them.

Questioning and shaping life

As a Lifestyle Entrepreneur, you create a life where you can take the talents, passions, interests and hobbies you have (as well as your education and work experience already gained), and design an entirely individual way of using them to earn a living. In my case, it is a lifestyle that has grown steadily towards bringing in as much as if I were putting in five days a week in a demanding employed job, yet I am far happier.

I have become a firm believer that you must have control over your future and the way that you are earning. Obviously, some people would say that you have that with a job, but if you become a Lifestyle Entrepreneur with multi-stream earnings, you potentially have much greater control, a stronger grip on what is going to earn you money and what you are going to do with your life.

I didn't really know what direction I wanted to take my career in when I was sixteen, which I know is true of so many people. It took a long time to figure out what I wanted to do, to be honest. So I followed the direction that seemed to present itself: my interest in science. While it was interesting and I went quite far with my studies, I realised it didn't feel like the way I wanted to spend my whole working life when I got a job with a media production company making online learning modules for GCSE science. But what could I do about that?

Despite being offered a good position a year or so later within the company, turning away from what was very possibly the route to a 'good, well-paid career' obviously did not look like good sense on paper! And I know my parents had thought that, after so much time studying science, I had a well-established career path to follow. Indeed, there was some hefty questioning when I announced I was giving it up to try to plough my own furrow! Luckily, I have parents who have mostly trusted me to make my own decisions and to learn from them.

It is perfectly possible to make very big money as a Lifestyle Entrepreneur, but that is not the philosophy behind the LE way, which is about finding or creating work that enriches your life and even the lives of others around you. It's important to note that the approach we talk about here is different to those that emphasise doing less work, aiming only for more money and pushing for early retirement.

Freelancer or Lifestyle Entrepreneur?

You may be asking the difference between the LE who is focused on multi-stream earning and the freelancer. There are some important distinctions:

Multi-stream earning is about shaping your passions to create a sustainable lifestyle, where you build your *streams* of work to fit around your life, whereas freelancing is often about pitching for a series of short-term jobs or 'commissions' that often have a finite end point and are not usually intended to continue and grow.

Multi-stream earners are constantly looking for ways to develop new lines of work that may be quite different to the others, so they are not single subject specialists like, say, a graphic designer.

Multi-stream earning incorporates both *passive* and *active* income streams (see chapter 3 on this). You could even become an investor for another business as a Lifestyle Entrepreneur. Freelance work can often end up fitting within the single employer-employee paradigm and hierarchy i.e. if you get a lot of work from one client, you can end up relying on them as your primary income source much like you would a traditional employer.

A successful life as a Lifestyle Entrepreneur

David Nicholson, 51, is a seasoned Lifestyle Entrepreneur who now earns around £100,000 a year. He always knew he didn't want a salaried office job, he says very firmly. 'So I spoke to people who were working as I wanted to do. I knew before I established myself that I wouldn't be able to earn the necessary income from writing as I do now. So as I had a suitable degree I used it do some tutoring in English, Maths, French, for about three years. 'At the same time I began to make approaches and get some writing work. I had edited a small magazine at university. At school they had encouraged the idea of entrepreneurship and set up a young business enterprise. So the idea that using one's own initiative to create work was in my mind.'

He worked hard at finding ideas suitable for different publications and used the *Writers and Artists' Yearbook*. 'I made every effort to meet and get to know journalists. As I began to get work and establish myself, journalist friends would pass on work they were too busy to do.

'There were up times and down times but I countered the effect of that somewhat by developing the knowledge to write on a broad range of subjects. I read textbooks on working for yourself that seemed helpful. You don't have to be an expert but to know how to research and find experts.'

So now he writes news and feature articles for a variety of publications and case studies for advertising copy. He works for the *Wall St Journal*, the *FT* and corporates such as ING. Then there are the political and corporate history books for companies. He also does social demographic profiling for marketing companies. He is content with what he earns, and the freedom and control over how he organises things strikes him as a very satisfactory state of affairs.

He has no doubt that choosing this way has given him the life he wants: 'I love the work and it is part of a package which includes freedom from having a boss, or answering to any corporate employer which becomes a greater privilege and joy the longer it lasts. Longevity in self-employment, where you make what is considered a healthy income, is regarded with surprise or disbelief by some contemporaries. So being approved of by one's peers is a measure of success.

'And I allow myself a good lifestyle. I take as many as 12 weeks holiday each year, travelling widely and staying in upmarket hotels, visiting tropical islands, the best ski resorts, cities like New York, Rio, Kuala Lumpur and attending sports events such as the football World Cup in Brazil. In London, I run a cricket team which plays in a dozen glamorous or picturesque locations and a vibrant and boozy lunch club. Only a fraction of this would be possible if I were an employee.'

The emotional side

When I worked full-time, with the draining business of commuting, the often uncomfortable switch between the way I was thinking in the office, possibly coming home with my head full of work stuff, maybe aggravated at being ordered to work in a way that didn't seem the most effective or likely to produce good results as my boss did, it impacted on my relationships.

With girlfriends, I was often tetchy and strung out for a while before we relaxed, and the stress I experienced at work could easily get in the way of happy, relaxed sex and languorous emotional talk, which is often a vital building block of a relationship.

These days, I certainly get stressed and frustrated at clients' demands at times: I can find myself working far longer hours than I want to and it can eat into time I have planned to do something relaxing with my wife. But I also know that when I have finished I can maybe take a day off and go to the beach with my wife, or I can sit up late watching a film and relaxing knowing an extra hour's lie-in won't matter.

And because my wife knows this way makes me happy, and that I see it as part of creating an integrated life with her, and one which can be re-shaped if we have children so that I can play a significant part in caring for them, she shrugs off the more difficult times as part of the deal.

Interestingly, even people who have invested several decades in building a career, rising up the ranks and believing this would be appreciated, find they are 'dug up from the roots and discarded' as one erstwhile woman executive in her 60s, now running a seaside cafe and knitting baby clothes for a local shop, described it. And understandably the loss of identity that goes with work, and the knowledge that getting a job as an employee over 50 can be extremely difficult, all too often leads to a sense of helplessness and depression.

So I am delighted in this book to have among the young LEs a good number of people who have shown very clearly that not only can they use skills and talents gathered through the years to create their own work, but they can find they are startlingly happier than they had been in a job so often with demanding hours, commuting and too little family time as part of the package. All this means my LE approach to living brings a good deal of spirit and closeness into our lives together.

2

DO I HAVE WHAT IT TAKES?

Do the qualities required to enjoy and be successful as a Lifestyle Entrepreneur reveal themselves when we are young? Certainly Owen Linderholm, writing for Yahoo Business on the success of older entrepreneurs, believes that entrepreneurial drive is inherent and we may see it manifest in young people and ear-mark them as future high-fliers, but at the same time that inherent drive can surface later, and to make the point he cites a remarkable bunch of very successful start-ups by people over 60.

If I look back, I see how much I enjoyed being an entrepreneur from a young age. I used to prepare packages to sell to passers-by on my doorstep of things like old VHS tapes, toys, chocolate desserts made from Rice Krispies, and computer games that I felt had passed their 'fun-by' date. In fact, anything I felt might have 'value' was up for grabs in my pre-pubescent entrepreneurial mind. Of course, the objects often had little more than the emotional value a six-year old attached to his toys at that time, but I felt like I was 'in business' and it was exciting.

Other moments in my life I now recognise were indicative of my drive to make money for myself: things like wanting to set up my computer game store with a friend when I was 11 as a means to have all the latest Mario games, exploring ways to get out of stuffing envelopes 9-5 when I had my holidays during sixth-form by selling books with one of those mail order services (for some unknown reason, that felt like a glamorous escape at the time!), and even starting my own diving school after I was inspired by a friend's uncle for whom I cooked and cleaned as an 18-year-old in exchange for diving classes. I liked the idea of having some control over what I was doing, doing something I was interested in, or at least being self-sufficient.

Early Indicators

I was never a Richard Branson character in the making, but I realised, increasingly, that the way I communicated with people who were intrigued by my selling habits had a lot to do with whether they were interested in the idea of entrepreneurial trading.

And what I learnt then, in embryonic form, I use today, although in a slightly more sophisticated form. But it is enjoying the interaction with people, even if they do not become customers, that is such a rich part of a lifestyle where you are designing what you do and how you do it.

The right time to start a business?

You wouldn't have thought the end of this millennium's first decade an auspicious time to go solo and start a business of your own. Britain was pitching into what was said to be the deepest recession since the 1930s, where unemployment for young people became so serious that even those with first class degrees, who would once have been virtually guaranteed work, found there was nothing for them.

But what we saw was a growing amount of creative thinking, as people of all ages began to think outside the box and start coming up with ideas for businesses of their own. And there have been some inspiring success stories of profits, social enterprise, and initiatives which showcase very well how work and home life can create a rewarding whole.

There may not be an ideal time to start a business, although obviously if you want to trade in goods or services, a buoyant economy and consumer confidence is helpful. But the skill to starting a business is to put effort into finding out whether there is likely to be a market for what you want to produce and whether you want to aim for something that will require large sales, or whether your dream is to do something smaller more specialised where a good deal of what you do in the beginning is likely to be getting yourself known.

Of course some bosses and organisations are a joy to work with, and can help you learn and progress in a career. Such a boss or colleagues may well enable you to understand how to work with others co-operatively, be part of a team working on a project, and try out your own ideas with someone senior to guide you. This can help a lot in building confidence in yourself that you will need to be a Lifestyle Entrepreneur.

So this may be a positive way for you begin and mature as a worker, but the idea of a single line of work, the same kind of working culture and lifestyle, can seem deadening and limiting to people with an entrepreneurial spirit.

Using workplace experience

I can only say if this is how you feel, make it your mission to research how others have moved into the LE way and think how you might translate their way for yourself. I did a good deal of research into filmmaking and what works musically to picture in my last job, and I transferred the ability I had developed in doing this to see how I might make my passion with music into an earning stream. I put all the time and effort I could into seeing what other composers were doing and who was making money; I explored the kind of soundtracks music libraries wanted; I communicated with people who ran those libraries and I put myself onto an Internet site where they were looking for people to score music for small films made by beginners and students.

I rightly guessed there would be no money in this but it was very good experience, looked great on my CV and, most importantly, I built relationships with people who have gone on to win various awards and prizes - some have gone on to produce more commercial work such as the film *Love at First Sight* which, after winning over 40 awards, is now selling on iTunes. Because I worked hard at getting the music scores exactly as they wanted, I have a strong relationship with those directors who are always looking to use me in their next paid projects.

Sara Charles graduated from college in 2007 but was disillusioned when she got work doing graphic design for large corporations because it did not fulfil the way she wanted to use her creativity. She began using her free time to create large prints, resplendent with birds and creatures, trees and flowers, and bold modern patterns. She set up an online storefront and began getting requests for throw pillows, decorative items and t-shirts printed with her patterns. She also saw that customers were willing to pay relatively high prices for something that was labour-intensive and involved skill, and which was not mass-produced. She has kept her business small so that she can devote time to doing the thing she really loves - designing - rather than concerning herself with hiring staff and managing a payroll. But she has been able to transform her hobby into a career and earn a good salary.

Thoroughly suited

Jonathan Self is something of a poster boy for the LE way. He is so thoroughly suited to what it offers. This man, exuding a breezy dynamism, has a decade and a half on me, and has been a Lifestyle Entrepreneur since the age of 21 when he started his first business in direct marketing, then sold it 11 years later without any clear idea what he would go on to do.

But he knew by then that he wanted to work as 'a generalist', trying his hand at different ways of earning a living and experimenting with his abilities. He left school at 16 with just a clutch of O-levels and thinks it very lucky that he developed several skills. He tells how it has been: 'In the early days I would work at anything to support myself, even if it was menial. That may not always be more interesting and certainly not more financially rewarding than being a full-time employee, but I calculated it was better than effectively selling my life to the firm. So for 25 years I have calculated how much money I need for a particular period and then tried to find ways of earning it that interest me.'

He knows well that many might think his cheery admission that 'I am not really motivated by money or external recognition so I have 'muddled along' without a 'proper' job for thirty years', curious in a man whose abilities include writing quality books and journalism, and founding socially responsible business *Honey's Real Dog Food*, which manufactures and sells ethically sourced organic dog food and numbers one royal household among his customers.

After all, with his smarts he would very probably have got himself rapidly up a career ladder and earning eye-watering sums. But Jonathan knew himself well enough to realise early on that he is fundamentally too unhappy with authority, and the risk of finding himself working for people he doesn't respect, to make that his goal. As well, he has seen too many friends who are senior employees but seem 'very frustrated with their single jobs'. So he views his own life as a success: 'I have absolute freedom to do what I want when I want it and waking up knowing that it truly gives me enormous pleasure and compensates completely for not having a bursting bank account and a Lamborghini.'

Office refusenik

Jonathan's words resonate with me, although it took me longer than it did him to identify myself as a LE candidate. My mother was remarking the other day what a hopeless refusenik I had been when it came to working in offices with a boss in charge. Even when I got a job that was certainly interesting and stimulating at times, I felt constrained because I wanted to go with ideas I had, and I quite often didn't agree with the way my boss wanted things done, nor did I like having to be there five days a week living with the politics and heavy sense of surveillance I felt in an office culture. I felt a lot of the time as though my life was being run without my consent.

Interestingly Lynda Gratton, professor of management at the London Business School, has been focusing on the question, 'What if money was no longer the most valuable asset a company could offer an employee?' and her point is that, as the population ages and people remain fit and active longer, the rewards that work brings other than simply earnings and status can be very important. She and her colleague Andrew Scott, in writing about the future of work, make the point that if we are going to need to support ourselves, very possibly into our 80s, while we will need money to live, this 'tangible asset' needs to be balanced by equally important intangible assets. And this is where designing our own work and lifestyle comes in. Scott and Gratton have seen clearly how important it is for older as well as younger people to find intellectual and creative engagement in what they do. Also, 'development potential,' which can be used outside of a single line of work, is important.

Hey, I find myself thinking, here are people who have researched their subject thoroughly, talking my language. That 'job description' fits so neatly into the LE way.

Rebellious spirit

Likewise, Michael Bihovsky, songwriter, author of musical theatre and singing teacher, thinks he would have far too much of a rebellious spirit to cope with life as a reliable employee.

'I don't respond well to being micro-managed by others, especially when they are less experienced than I am and don't use common sense. And the great virtue is I have no fear of losing my jobs, because I don't have a boss to fire me. I have many clients for many things, and we have a truly wonderful working relationship. And if we didn't, I could always just walk out the door! Or they could walk out the door, and I'd have dozens of other clients to fall back on.'

Michael almost vibrates with enthusiasm as he runs through a list of the different ways he earns a living, telling first of the comedy musical he has written, based on his own experience of having a number of distressing food allergies, 'One More Grain....'. He carried on a relentless Facebook promotion and raised more than 104% of the asked for $10,000 through Kickstarter.

Then there is the acting and songwriting Michael teaches, which bring in the largest part of his income. From time to time he is employed by a performing company to act or sing himself. Oh, and there are the short musical films he has written and produced, funding and working on them himself, and there's no cracking his cheery conviction that one day he will hit the big time.

So his life is a patchwork of earning streams for which he uses different skills he has developed, and he gives a small shudder at the idea of confining himself to just one line of work. Nor can he imagine wanting a job within an organisation where he does not control his own destiny. That, anyway is ruled out he says, because he has a chronic connective tissue disorder - Ehlers-Danlos Syndrome - which saps his energy so thoroughly that he is incapacitated for days or even weeks sometimes and he asks wryly: 'What boss will put up with that?'

And resourceful to the last, from this unhappy situation Michael has pulled another earning stream: he is writing medical articles and a book on the topic of 'human brokenness'.

He is clear, too, why multi-stream earning is his chosen way. 'I would get extremely bored doing the same thing every day. Doing multiple jobs keeps me from becoming saturated with any one task. Each area influences the other. For instance being a teacher has made me a far better director, and being an actor has made me a better writer. Content for my artistic creations has come from being a chronic disease activist. And so on.'

Frankly you could be forgiven for wishing the spirited 27-year-old all the best with his shooting star ideas, while seeing him as the exception who will never be the rule. But you would be very wrong.

Michael is just one of a steadily growing number of go-it-aloners with a portfolio of work which is different to the traditional idea of freelance jobs, because each income stream is developed as one strand of a sustainable job for the foreseeable future. It is a way of earning a living where each strand can be supported by and / or support the other streams. It is also, for many, a stimulating way of flexing a variety of creative muscles rather than being limited to a single work involvement. 'I have little financial security, which can be unnerving, but I have succeeded every year for the past five in doubling my own income.'

There are good reasons why this may be a particularly suitable way for younger generations. For them the workplace has changed dramatically in the past couple of years. We have seen soaring youth unemployment, unpaid internships and apprenticeships that don't actually lead to work, and a situation where demand for work has given employers the power to cut back what may be paid, and to alter workplace safeguards and conditions. So aside from the positive impulse to set up our own earning streams, it may be necessary to find a way to do so.

Olderpreneurs

That said, there are also many mid and later-lifers who become Lifestyle Entrepreneurs. The reason may be redundancy, or retirement, but it can also be the desire to change course, explore various business ideas and try new ways to earn. 'The level of self-employment in the 50-plus age group is about 1 in 5, and government figures show that the number of pensioners starting a business has increased steadily', says Nick Smurthwaite, author of an article for *Age UK* on the phenomenon.

Collected experience and expertise means that this group of start-up entrepreneurs with their years of work experience is likely to succeed, with over 70% starting businesses lasting more than 5 years. But as with the young, embarking on a steep learning curve as they pitch into start-ups and grassroots initiatives, the same ingredients are needed whatever your maturity: passion, excitement and a desire to use new skills.

No clear plan - but a happy outcome

The bright, warm voice of Matt Stone, 50, introduces a man who sees how the years he spent in a challenging job have done much to help the way he works now. In his mid 30s, he quit his job in international marketing for Rolls-Royce & Bentley and eventually set up a run of digital projects, each an earning stream. It was a brave thing to do, he knows. He had a prestigious position as global head of Marketing Communications for the iconic motor brands, following a career in sales and marketing with Saab in the formative years and later Toyota and Lexus.

He explains: 'I enjoyed car sales and marketing and they were great jobs to talk about at a dinner party. But the bottom line was I worked extremely hard for someone else. I had done it for 15 years and it hit me one day that I felt like a small cog in a big wheel. Then came the wake up call when with the emergence of the Internet in the 90s which I saw as a unique business opportunity and made the case for taking Bentley online for the first time in its history. But not only were there no thanks, more than one board member was dismissive about any commercial success there might be for a digital channel in the future...I realised they didn't trust or value me so why was I putting all my effort and ability into building their business?'

So he began by setting up a business called ROI, offering marketing consultancy to big brands. 'I didn't have a clear plan, and I remember getting on the phone in Winchester where I was based, ringing around contacts, making up to 30 calls a day. Enough people were interested that I realised I had a viable idea and I still advise brands to this day. But I also began working in a more specialist way, creating disruptive digital business models for early stage businesses. He started small and with some successes along the way was able to increase the risk and the returns with each venture. This in turn meant the ability to work with better and better people, which has proven to be the catalyst for longstanding business success. 'Always work with people smarter than you' is a mantra he lives by.

He also learned how, when you work for yourself, you need to be agile enough if a great idea comes along, and to stick with it, although he warns: 'This is not for the fainthearted. I have often worked 70 - 80 hours a week and at weekends because with digital the "shop never closes".'

Four years ago one such great opportunity did present itself. Matt was at a charity dinner on a table with Gary Lineker and he got talking with a friend of Gary's about how best to bring down the cost of car insurance for young drivers. Finding a way to improve their driving and in doing so reduce the loading that the young attract because they are collectively seen as high risk. They came up with the idea of ingenie, a digital brand which resonated with young drivers. A black box that gives precise data on how a young person is driving and a 'traffic light' app so that both the driver and parents know how well their son or child is driving, with the app acting as a co-pilot to help them improve and drive more safely.

'It is reassuring for parents but also it helps young drivers to realise if they are driving badly and importantly to treat them as individuals and help them to drive more safely.' says Matt.

Lineker invested in ingenie and Sir Frank Williams, founder and team principal of the Williams Formula One racing team, who is tetraplegic following a crash in France, gave it his early backing. It was successful enough to be valued at over £100 million after less than two years' trading.

Matt's interest in cars has led to a new venture and intended earning stream. A service to help people - and women particularly whom he believes are sometimes patronised in car dealerships - to 'try and buy' a car without having to go to a car showroom or be looked after by a salesperson whose primary interest may just be to get a commission. When he's not advising or creating start-ups, he's mentoring wannabe entrepreneurs at the Accelerator Academy.

Mindset

I have suffered frequently from lack of confidence, feeling inadequate or rejected when my projects do not go as well as I had hoped or when I cannot meet a client's wishes, when a piece of work is refused because it apparently doesn't fit the brief, when a piece of music I have sweated over gets an unenthusiastic response or, as is common in the advertising world, receives no response at all. And it is hard. This may be the time you want to throw it all in, wish there was a work colleague around to unload on to or seek guidance or solace, but if, as I do, you work on your own, then you have to learn to deal with these feelings.

Because we have taken the bold step of going it alone, we do not automatically shed the thin skins, the difficult existential feelings, the fears of not being approved of that so many of us have in our goal and status oriented society. I used to think it was just we relative youngsters who felt that way, but I now know how the feelings people of all different ages and stages. But dealing with these can be easier than if you are in an office being humiliated in front of others because your superior is displeased or because a client chooses not to use the work you did and you never understand why. You learn to adapt and that, in my opinion, is one of the most valuable skills you can develop in life.

Are you doing your best?

An important first step if you do hit a bad patch or seem no longer to be in demand is to eyeball your work as clearly and critically as you can. Be honest with yourself about whether you have given it your best shot, or whether you thought you could get away with cutting corners. And if you decide you have done so, it may feel right to go to whoever you were doing it for and say you do not feel happy with what you have done so could you re-do it. This way you may re-build a potentially lost relationship. It is also important to feel able to confront situations that have gone wrong and apologise when necessary.

30-year old multi-stream earner Natalia Talkowska, who does financial and editorial work for a range of clients, talks of how: 'In the beginning when I faced rejection if I applied for work I took it very emotionally and could only see it as negative and I would not want to go back to the person who had turned me down even if I might have something to offer in future.

'But I have trained myself to face up. Now, I do a proposal and I always ask for feedback. I want to know the real reason why I didn't get the work because that will help me improve things next time and then I move forward to other opportunities.'

Natalia believes connecting with clients is the heart of it all.

'There are different tools to help you focus on your clients but you need to connect with them on every level, don't start talking about business straight away. I always find it better to approach people's wishes in a personal way. I try to keep my clients happy, have a conversation with them.

'With time I have developed a lot more confidence and time management skills but I also try to keep a balance between my personal and professional lives because what's the point of having these successes when you haven't got anyone to share them with, but also having this balance it really helps your mind and makes you happier.'

Do not let one rejection, when there have been 20 successful experiences, become the dominating one. Cultivate a friend or mentor who will give support and comfort but also help you see if you have gone wrong. There are assertiveness and resilience courses, and counselling online and in person if you feel the need of some expert help.

Self-image

Lucy McCarraher, writer, editor and publisher, who set up Rethink Press, takes a view on how to create a sound psychological mindset. 'Ideally, you really need to love what you do and cultivate a self image which includes seeing yourself as creative or entrepreneurial. An image of yourself as enjoying rather than fearing risk-taking. You need to believe everything is going to work out somehow.'

Lucy is sure that having chosen to be in charge of her own business, and the place where the buck stops, makes her 'an eternal optimist. I am driven by always believing this is the new activity that is going to be the one [to] make me some money. The pleasure of multi-stream earning is that there is always that possibility...I am in tune with William Congreve who wrote in Love for Love: "Uncertainty and expectation are the joys of life. Security is an insipid thing."'

Ignoring the naysayers

For many years I had accepted that earning a living through music was impossible because of how hard everyone told me it was. And they are right: it is hard. Hard but not impossible, and that is what I have found as slowly, but fairly steadily, my passion for music is becoming a growing income stream.

But if I had listened to the naysayers, those who pointed to all the reasons it was a lunatic notion to believe I could usefully invest time in composing music and selling it, I would have given up the idea before I tested my ability and the response of the market. To my surprise, music showed itself to be a very valid option for supporting my lifestyle.

The exciting thing was that the types of audio work I intended to do would allow me to work on zero-budget projects like *Rocket*, a short film about a dog who builds a rocket to go to space, that I scored for filmmakers Jennifer Sheridan and Matthew Markham. Projects like this satisfy my soul because I love writing music to picture and often it leads on to other interesting opportunities. They make me *feel* as if I have been paid because the work is so satisfying. In this case, *Rocket* actually won the *Virgin Media Shorts* grand prize of £30,000 which we used to fund the next project with support of the *British Film Industry* (BFI), so those unpaid opportunities can actually lead to paid opportunities as well.

I so often hear the downbeat message being delivered to those who want to find their own way, all the reasons about why it is too risky, that there's no demand, no interest or even that an idea is plain 'shit'. But if you are in a position to take a few weeks or even months to test the water with your idea, while maybe doing a job like bar work which will not take up all your creative energy and thought processes, then you can bring in enough cash to support yourself while actually refining and testing your ideas out, which is a fundamental part of becoming an LE.

A friend once told me 'there is a market for everything' and I think he was pretty much right. I see it all the time as I continue to build additional income streams and that some of them have a paying audience even surprises me sometimes! It is just possible that the naysayers wish they dared to do it themselves and envy your bravado in becoming a Lifestyle Entrepreneur.

3

WE ALL HAVE SKILLS - IDENTIFY YOURS

Passion is what drives Kimberley Pryor, 26, and she says it several times. It's the thing that means you will find her at 7.30 a.m. in a City of London coffee house with her laptop, deep into digital constructs for personal enterprises that she intends to build into a multi-stream business in due course. She is in the early stages of her working life and is glad of a full-time job as a paid employee with a charity, which she enjoys, while she attempts to build the businesses.

Her skills as a digital producer, managing digital projects from speccing and requirement gathering through to implementation, testing and continued improvements, are the basis of all she does. She spends much time with designers, copywriters and developers to make digital ideas become reality.

'My salaried day job at a London blood cancer charity takes up the majority of my time. Outside work hours I work on Novlr, an online novel writing software, which I run with a friend, Thomas, who shares my view that work and play should go together. I also run a spoken word poetry night in London, again with Thomas. Lastly, I pick up projects here and there! When people know you can code, you are offered work regularly. Better still, when you get known for working well and being thorough, you are offered more work and it gives confidence to see a future working for myself.'

A starting point for becoming a Lifestyle Entrepreneur is to identify where your abilities, skills and interests could be taken if you wanted them to bring in an income. Obviously some may excite you but probably not make a lot of money - at least at first - but initially what you need to do is get your mind thinking in a lateral way that can unleash creative imagination.

I started looking at what skills I could offer and monetize a number of years ago because it enabled me to spend more time with my Spanish girlfriend in Seville. But before that, I was working as a production assistant for a digital agency producing didactic material for kids learning GCSE science as part of an online initiative the BBC had funded in the UK. That gave me transferable skills for digital work and I was able to use these with my web work, research, cold-calling, and also my music. Once you realise the potential you have to earn from a variety of skills, it's just a matter of getting your hands dirty trying things out and enjoying the experience of exploring the possibilities.

I can hear you thinking, this is all very well, but I don't have skills outside the job I trained for. I might love the idea of being a Lifestyle Entrepreneur except that I would probably end up pacing the streets with my hand outstretched asking for a bob or two.

What skills do you have?

But is this really true? What are your interests, the passions you indulge in when there is free time? The hobbies you have only ever dabbled in, abilities you have gained through living your life (whether it is as seemingly insignificant as weeding a neighbour's garden or babysitting their children)? How about repairing someone's car, making curtains for them or sorting out their computer problems because you have techie knowledge that they do not? If you are a skilled hill walker you might organise weekends for groups going to special places you have discovered. All of these have the potential to be turned into earning streams, the challenge is for you to work out how to do this.

There are probably essential tasks that are part of running your home and life such as cleaning, washing and ironing, taking and collecting children from school. These have the potential to be earning streams if, for example, you wanted to set up a cleaning service, or a taxi service taking and delivering children to school for people who have to go to work too early to take their own.

Most of us do not stop to think about how many skills we have, what we are good at outside our chosen career or work, but it can be surprising how many there are when you stop having a cemented division between work and everything else you do. Change the mindset and it may be surprising what you come up with.

If you think about your experiences up until now, you've been constantly learning and building your knowledge about certain things. You know more than the person next to you about subject X which often means you are an 'expert' in their eyes, even if you haven't realised it yet. That's a profitable skill that can be capitalised on.

As an exercise, try writing down the enjoyable things you do during any given week. It is valuable to set aside time when you will not be interrupted or have other things on your mind that will intrude, and brainstorm with yourself thinking about every and any way the things you would like to do could become a viable way of earning a living.

Simon Ratcliffe, an IT consultant who has been self employed for 23 years, has had several business ventures and gives talks to young people about working for themselves. He also believes that a person needs to want to work for themself, something I've done by spending the last two years of my employment going to courses and preparing for self-employment.

It was frustration at not finding a decent beer when they went for a drink after work in their local pubs that set William Harris, 23, Andrew Birkby, 26, and Jaega Wise, 25, discussing how they might make their own. It was a joke at first, but then it began to seem a real possibility. There is a collective snort of laughter at the improbability of such a thing - that they should have a go at creating an ale themselves - but William remembers the determination that took root: 'I became obsessed with making this happen.'

Ten years later they are based in London running their own *Wild Card Brewery* and producing a beer that won the *Drink Britain* beer of the month award, and they have their own Brewery Tap Bar, open at weekends. Andrew thinks it the best thing he could have done: 'Following your dream is an act of faith and when that comes into being work is pleasure.'

The mind map

One of the most effective ways of exploring where I could take a particular skill, subject, passion, is to create mind maps. The British memory expert and popular-psychology author Tony Buzan advocated and, in fact, coined the term. Mind Maps are a kind of 'tree diagram' often illustrated with colours with a central concept in the middle and sub-items branching off. While working as a journalist for a charity magazine, I interviewed Tony Buzan, who explained how mind maps help you remember things better and organise your thoughts efficiently.

I put one together based on the types of things that interest me, the services and crafts I could offer businesses or individuals and some other things I'm interested in and which I could use profitably.

As my main passion is music, but web development is something I'm well versed in, you can see there are a lot of branches stemming from these areas. And the point of a mind map is to see how many off-shoots you can identify that you might develop into a small or large earning stream.

I graduated in biology, so, aside from music and web work, there are a variety of things I could offer stemming from this, such as carrying out basic research, tutoring students, guest blogging for specialty websites or even writing my own educational material to sell as an eBook or online subscription course with modules.

Susan Noble

Suzanne Noble, 53, developed her Lifestyle Entrepreneur way of

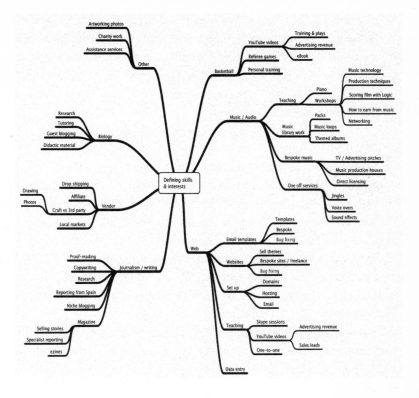

living after working in single careers. First, she pursued the dream, after university, of getting into film production and she succeeded in getting commissioned to do a series for Channel Four. Disillusion came fast. 'That was a powerful insight into what a tough competitive world TV is and how little personal say or control you have over what you do. I realised it was not the way I wanted to live. I got married at this time and my husband and I set up our own PR company which worked as I was having babies as well. We made a success of that and earned a lot of money.'

Then her marriage broke down and her husband took the business over. Suzanne had money earned which she used to embark on running a working life to suit her needs and wishes.

'I started by designing baby slings and was able to fund having them made in India. They sold fairly well but I needed a further income stream.' She researched a while and decided that there was a niche for a line of sex toys very different to the kind of thing already being sold. She designed these and had them made up but could not find a market: 'I had to count that as a lost leader. But I had made connections in the area and I immediately had another idea to make sex education films'.

She hired a health editor of *Cosmopolitan* magazine and, with earnings from the PR business and selling a home she was in a position to invest £70,000 in the films.

She tells how it was. 'I found couples willing to talk about their great sex lives and be filmed. We shot them on three cameras. I made two videos which were a great success and they still bring in some money. I realised there was a market for more work around sex and so I wrote two novels about my own sexual adventures, under a pseudonym to protect my children, and within two weeks of contacting agents I had a contract. They sold well, too.'

You sense that all Suzanne's zest goes into being an entrepreneurial businesswoman and she uses her enormous energy and wit to keep creating new earning streams. Among her present income streams are a brother and sister graphic artist team who she took on, introduced them to an agent and got a big publishing contract for them. She uses her PR skills helping with Oink a kind of PayPal for children. She works with someone producing a children's book and there is work for the charity Soldier On which is largely a philanthropic job with a small fee. And her latest venture is the creation of an app Frugl for people wanting to enjoy London on a low budget with all kinds of activities all £10 and under.

Sharpening your skills

You may need to build on your skills before you can start earning an income stream from them. Whether you do that 'on the job,' as I did when writing stock music, or decide to take a course, the important thing is to identify what it is you need to excel in for people to take you seriously.

By checking for demand, you'll get some idea. And regardless of whether you feel you have all the skills you need already, you should try to continually improve your skill set so you can provide more value to your customers.

Someone who consistently improves his or her skills will inevitably be more attractive than someone who is offering less expertise for the same money. Even if you feel you are able enough to set up selling a product or service, you need to realise that we live in a work world where new ideas, new technology, new approaches are constantly being devised and if you don't keep up with the game, an earning stream that has done perfectly well may begin losing ground if you do not have the most modern skills or keep an eye on trends and developments.

In my case, for my web work, I have had to constantly upgrade my knowledge of my existing programming skills and website design standards, and learn new systems and programming languages to meet clients' demands. This can often entail seeking help from someone who has the knowledge you need and should be seen as an investment if it will help you get more work or potential clients as a result.

There are a multitude of people who offer training programmes on just about any topic, from technical know-how and writing for publications, to the latest take on yoga, cookery, interior design and car maintenance. Many courses can be bought online, self-help and DIY books can be found in your local library or you may find a specialist with a blog that is informative. You might also find the author of the blog would be willing to help you individually for a small fee, or even for free.

One of the most rewarding things about the LE world, I find, is how willing people are to help each other and I have had many online and offline conversations. One musician in particular, Matt Harris, whose work I admire hugely, became something of a mentor after I approached him for help and is now a friend as well, with whom I often meet up and chat with into the wee hours of the morning, either online or in person when I visit him in his Cardiff home town.

Another way of skilling up is to go to conferences, talks and workshops on your chosen subject. The best of these can give you a good toolkit for building on your work stream, and it is very helpful to network with other people with the same interest and with whom you may be able to exchange information and ideas.

Reading books, watching videos (like tutorials on YouTube), downloading eBooks, podcasts and radio interviews are also good and often free or inexpensive ways of building on skills.

Is there a market?

There will be some things on your list of skills from which it may be difficult to create an income outside of the workplace. Pig farming while living in a city comes, randomly, to mind. But it can also be true of banking, being a barrister, a car manufacturer, or even a personal assistant depending on your situation, so think hard about how and where you would trade your skills.

Finding a niche market and getting known as THE person for a certain kind of goods, from publicity leaflets, a particular style of photography, a magician with state of the art tricks etc. can help you become a good earner and provide you with the security of knowing there are not thousands of other people threatening to undercut you.

You should ask yourself if your ideas are complicated to implement, expensive, or have little commercial demand. A bit of market research is essential before you create your wonderful wares and find they just are not what's wanted. If you want to create, say, gluten-free bread and cakes you need to see who else is doing this, where they sell, if possible how well they do, and try to identify a niche where you might make an unusual idea work. If you are really determined it is surprising how many things there is a market for, but getting in front of the right eyes or being heard among the masses can sometimes be the biggest hurdle.

Take Helena Appio. She loves needlework and started creating felt animals as a hobby. Acquaintances began ordering them and paying well for the intricately made ornaments so she has developed that ad hoc beginning into a business. She approached an upmarket shop in central London where they get orders for her felt dogs and often people order them in the design of their own much loved pet. She plans to extend this earning stream into giving workshops in making felt animals in her home.

Being inventive

The belief that she could live from creating different income streams came from watching her Nigerian mother making a living by being hugely inventive when she moved from a sheltered home in the UK to live in Africa where things were very basic. 'She quickly learned to turn her hand to doing almost anything and she used this to make necessary money.'

Helena worked for the BBC for 12 years but resigned because there were so many other things she wanted to do and there was never time. She uses the skills developed in this job to work part-time for a documentary company, along with teaching in film school and being an external examiner at the Open University. Then as a much-admired creator of cakes decorated with images to order, she has been able to turn this into another growing income stream. Next move was Hong Kong to be with her husband as he got a job there, but she negotiated to continue working on developing a film with a UK based company, when she went in 2015.

Some passions or ideas may have a longer trajectory than those that are straightforward or clearly in demand. You need to think about doing some preparation, producing a business plan (even if just a small one) and whether you need an investment (be it time or money) to be able to put your plan into action.

Find a niche

We have seen how Helena created a niche for the felt animals she was making as a hobby and creating a niche product is one way you may make a name for yourself in a crowded market. For instance, if Helena had chosen quick turnover, low price stuffed toys to make, the chances are she would have been less successful because it is already such a crowded market and there would have been nothing to make Helena's products stand out. Remember, The more specific you become with your offerings, the less chance there is of competition. In addition, if you can clearly identify your target audience it will help you with your marketing considerably.

Selling online is a popular way to at least start as you do not need the overheads of an office or shop. To do this you need to be part of a marketplace or have a really effective, eye-catching website that will act as a shop front, as well as to learn how to pull in customers.

If you are running a small local market stall selling home-grown produce or taxi-ing children around (to do anything with children you will need to be police checked) where leafleting and word of mouth work well for you, you may not see the need of a website. But most people who want to get known for what they are selling, and who want to establish themselves as a brand, find they need a website if not for anything else than as an online 'business card' or brochure of your services.

Your website

If you plan to employ an expert to create your website, it is obviously worth looking around to see who makes the kind of website you want. Alternatively, look at websites that other people with a similar trade to yours have and find out who created them. If your needs are simple i.e. you just want a public-facing space to showcase your work, offer information about your services or a way for people to get in touch, then there are plenty of cheap resources out there that will let you do so within your budget.

For example, Squarespace (squarespace.com) offers beautifully designed templates and web hosting for a monthly fee meaning you can save having to get a custom design done by a web developer, paying separately for hosting every month and any maintenance that comes with having a website (remember, a website is like a car and needs regular looking after). However, they don't offer email hosting which can be a deal-breaker for some people.

Other popular options are Weebly (weebly.com), Wix (wix.com), Virb (virb.com), Strikingly (strikingly.com) Tumblr (tumblr.com) and Wordpress.com (which is different to Wordpress.org where you download their software to install on your hosting as opposed to the former which hosts the software for you). Just remember, that email hosting is often not offered with these 'hosted' solutions as they're called, so to have branded email like me@mydomain.com, you'll need to purchase that separately or just make do with a free service like Gmail.

If you're up-to-speed with technology, another option is to purchase a website theme from a store like ThemeForest (themeforest.net), get some hosting from a site like Hostgator (hostgator.com), and learn how to install that website by yourself. It's more involved, but can be a cheap way to get all the benefits of a full hosting package like hosted email and being able to run multiple sites off one hosting package.

Focus on purpose

Something you'll want to be careful of when creating your own site is making sure it fulfils its purpose. What I mean by that is I've seen countless clients of mine think they need more than they actually do at the start of a project. Unless you're selling physical or digital products online, or a website is mission-critical to your business and depends on complex coding, you can probably get up and running quickly with services like Squarespace or Weebly.

However, if you are entering the realm of e-commerce (selling digital or physical products via your website), it's worth investing in something that will give you the tools you need and provide support when you need it. Having researched the options and built various sites, for hosted solutions I tend to recommend Shopify (shopify.com) as it simplifies and solves a lot of the problems you'll encounter in e-commerce.

Selling online

If you are thinking about setting up a website to sell something, then it's worth learning a bit about Internet Marketing (IM). Going into the details of IM would be a book in itself and is an area that changes very fast (sometimes within weeks or a single month as search engines change the way they list results), but it's important as it's the way you'll reach your customers and therefore make sales.

You'll want to research a bit about IM best practices or hire someone to take care of marketing for you, but using tools like Google's keyword planner (adwords.google.com/KeywordPlanner) to find niche specific keywords and see if anyone is interested or is searching for things in your niche can be very useful, if not fundamental, in finding out if your idea has legs online.

One of the best practices that Google is currently favouring, for example, is to isolate what are called 'longtail keywords' and use them in content on your website, like in an article on a blog. Longtail keywords are essentially highly-focused sentences with keywords that people type into search engines to find what they're looking for. Google's aim with prioritising sites that use them is to improve their search results by displaying accurately relevant website links.

For example, you might use something like 'Messi's best football tricks at Barcelona football club' as opposed to just 'football skills' which is too general and won't bring in 'targeted traffic,' as it's called. If your blog was about teaching football skills and you had an article about Barcelona's star Lionel Messi and his skills, this could bring in potential customers who you could sell things to, like a video course on how to pull off the coolest football tricks known to mankind, or an eBook on how to start your own football tricks academy locally. If you get a lot of traffic, you might even make some money off advertising by embedding some Google Ads into the sidebar of your blog and earning every time someone clicks on an advert. For a guide on how to use

KeywordPlanner, Neil Patel has some good tips here: quicksprout.com/university/how-to-use-google-keyword-planning-tool.

Football skills is just one example of course, but you could do the same with almost any specialist area you're interested in by testing topics from 'caring for your orchid in cold climates' if you were a gardener, to 'how to research the most newsworthy content for podcasts' if you worked in journalism, 'best practices for pitching your idea to venture capitalists' if you worked in start ups, or even 'the medicinal qualities of marijuana' if that is your thing (you might not be surprised to hear that one is already out there!).

Breaking things down

I am going to use my own experience to illustrate how you might approach breaking down your experience into different ways of earning. When I did my Masters in Science Communication, I gained experience writing for a few publications, I feel confident I could offer a range of services such as:

Science journalism
Pitching articles for newspapers, magazines, blogs etc.
Copywriting for websites and trade publications
Providing workshops on how to write for the web
Reporting from Spain for English-speaking news outputs
Proofreading
Transcribing

So you can see how a single degree offered me a whole range of earning possibilities. But the list doesn't stop there. If I think of my education outside my degree, there are a bunch of other things I learned that offer potential earning avenues. For example, when I was 21 I took a couple of month-long courses at Queen's Park New Media Centre in web design and music production. Those two (free) courses along with an interest in both subjects gave me a bunch of skills that I still use today to generate income:

- Building and designing websites with HTML, CSS, PHP, JavaScript and a couple of other web programming languages
- UX design - an area (or even a whole industry within) website development that helps you understand and create better experiences for visitors
- Coding email newsletters
- How to compose, mix and master electronic music in Logic and Pro Tools (both popular programs for making music)
- Recording techniques, working in a studio and how to market your music

Will it make me money?

You can see how breaking your talents down can help you explore where they might lead. However, you may have to look at your overall skills and then separate them as profitable or non-profitable if you want to make money.

For example, if you have worked in office administration you have a variety of skills to offer:

Telesales
Bookkeeping
Personal assistant
Events scheduling
Inventory management
Project management
Recognising trends in a sector
Working with programs like Excel, Powerpoint & Word

Once you've identified some of your skills, you can test whether they are real income earners by looking at the competition and asking yourself if there is a market for those skills. And more often than not, there is indeed a market.

When I analysed it, I realised how many things I was learning and using in my work as a web developer and how they could quite easily translate into other, different earning streams if I wanted to develop them:

- Coding: when I was coding I was obliged to adopt strict and fairly sophisticated organisational skills
- Learning a language: I was learning Spanish at the time and coding essentially involves learning another language
- Mathematical calculations: even basic algebra, addition, subtraction etc. has been very useful in learning to create websites and run the 'accounting' side of my income streams
- Personal relations: any business relies on making good relationships with the people who you work with, so social skills need to be developed if you lack them
- Basic computer skills such as word processing, using the Internet, email management etc. The current generation will be up to speed with this, but if you don't know how to use a computer and want to work online, you'll need to develop that skill as it's essential
- Being available: making oneself available when your clients need you will make you much more attractive than competitors. I can't tell you the number of times I've picked up work because someone else has been slack communicating with their client

When defining your skills, always keep in mind who you're trying to attract and whether it's a skill that people will think is worth paying for. Things like 'making the best chocolate cake' is only going to be of interest to people who want to buy your cakes, not the busy office professional who needs his receipts organised.

And remember that the more specific you can be about what you're offering, the more clearly you will be able to identify your target audience which will help you with your marketing.

Keep learning
Much like sharpening your skills, recognising new skills learned is

also a constant process. This is something that develops and evolves over time, meaning you increase your value to the people who need your skills. Although that sounds obvious, many people forget that as you improve and expand your abilities over time, you can also charge more money as you're carrying out more skilled work.

What to call yourself

Names can mean a lot, just ask Jack Cator, founder and sole owner of the Virtual Private Network (VPN) service *Hide My Ass* (HMA), who sold his business for a cool 60 million dollars to the software group AVG in 2015. Cator highlights how HMA hasn't only been successful because of the service offered: 'Our name has helped massively too...people are amused by it - once you hear it, you can't possibly forget it.'

It may be worthwhile finding a title for what you do that is not just run of the mill. So for instance if you worked in office admin-istration, you could call yourself something unusual like a 'Bureaucracy Manager' or 'Event Scheduling Assistant'. Coining slightly unusual terms often prompts people to find out more about what you are actually offering, especially if it sounds as though it is solving a problem someone needs sorted such as organising records or book keeping.

Of course, you shouldn't lie about what you're capable of, but often but a job will lend itself to many skills and you should capitalize on that when defining the skills you can offer.

Passive and active earning

The term 'passive income' is bandied around quite a lot on the Internet and is often described as an income stream that you 'set and forget'. That is, you do the work of creating something once (like writing an eBook), set up a way for it to sell (like putting it on the Amazon Kindle store) and then you just sit back and watch the money roll in 'passively'.

Sounds great right? While it's totally possible to earn this way, it's often not as simple as it sounds. The word 'passive' is a bit of misnomer because, as you can imagine, earning in the background with no effort is an attractive concept, which means there are lots of people doing the same and all of them are shouting for people's attention. That means you actually need to *continually* work quite hard when earning passively with things like marketing to reach a market that will buy your service or product. But the basic concept of passive earning is that you do the work first and then continue to profit from that effort later.

Examples of passive earning with which most of us are probably familiar include things like royalties earned by musicians, book authors, performers and so on, where they may have been paid for their initial work, but get further payments if the work is re-used publicly. Other sources of passive income include eBooks, mobile phone apps, ringtones, online software services like accounting and invoicing software, and even subscription-based tutorial sites where you can pay a monthly fee to access learning resources on anything from botany and how to make pizza to coding websites and how to play guitar. Most often, it's an *automated* way to generate income.

'Active' earning, on the other hand, is a more traditional way of bringing in income. You could see it as the typical freelancer or consultant approach to working in that you get commissioned to do a job for a client that you work for, invoice for it and then get paid (usually a month or so later). In most cases, it involves one-off jobs or there is a finite end-point on the horizon for all the work involved. This is how many sole traders and small 'one-man/woman' businesses earn a living.

For example, the voice-over work I do brings in earnings from each job and at the same time puts me in touch with a large number of other entrepreneurs who regularly employ me. This is an example of an 'active' income stream which does not bring repeat earnings per se, but does lead me to new customers and further 'one-off' jobs.

Mixing passive with active

Passive income is becoming an ever larger part of the way LEs earn as it provides a buffer for your earnings when active income streams are a bit thin on the ground. Even when you're constantly scouting for new opportunities, client work comes and goes and any freelancer can attest to how some months can subsequently become particularly tough financially.

Passive income can fill the gap and provide the 'stability' in your LE salary, so getting the balance between passive and active income streams can really provide you with peace of mind. However, because passive earning can be so volatile, I wouldn't recommend it as a sole source of income. If you sell textile patterns on a marketplace, for example, and then suddenly the patterns you sell become unfashionable or Google makes you disappear from search results or the market just becomes saturated with competitors, then your income from that can dwindle fast.

This actually happened recently with my earnings from selling royalty-free music on various marketplaces due to Google penalising the marketplaces I sell on and the affiliate sites that link to it for having 'thin' content. The drop in traffic (and therefore sales) has been quite drastic, but because this passive income is not my sole source of money and I have multiple passive income streams, I have been able to ride the downturn relatively easily.

Show me the money

To date, my passive earnings are around $1,000 to $2,000 per month (most marketplaces sell in USD) and are growing continually as I add new ones or improve my existing set ups. That might be via things like mixing my music better, marketing through social media or reaching out to new customers directly.

These streams are much slower to build up and they ebb and flow each month, which means I cannot rely on them entirely, but combined with the active streams, I have been reaching £5,000 to £7,000 gross income on a 'good' month and £1,000 on a 'bad' month. Other than my mortgage at this point, my overheads are low meaning I can pay the bills and other costs quite easily. Although earning this way may look risky at the beginning, it is actually a very stable way to earn once you get going.

Considered one of the 'celebrities' of the passive income world, Pat Flynn is a part-time dad and part-time Internet entrepreneur who runs the blog www.smartpassiveincome.com. Flynn publishes his earnings in a report each month along with tips and tutorials on how to earn passive income through various methods like affiliate websites (which we'll talk about in more depth later) and building websites and apps. Flynn says:

'I didn't win the lottery, I don't drive a fancy car, and I'm not a millionaire. What I do have is a beautiful wife, two amazing children, a loving family, awesome friends, and a line of work that allows me to spend most of my time with them.'

As is common on these types of sites, there is a clear 'persona' behind his narrative. Much of his success as a passive income earner comes from people feeling they know and trust him and see him as an authority on the subject of passive income.

Visitors to the site follow the affiliate links to products and services he endorses throughout his site (from which Flynn earns a commission). He continually provides free and useful information through things like podcasts and blog posts and runs a variety of other endeavours that also bring him passive income.

Passive Earning Sites

Earning a passive income from digital products can be a highly lucrative project. One of the more popular platforms I sell on called Envato (envato.com) is one of a multitude of marketplaces where you can sell almost anything digital.

AudioJungle (audiojungle.net) is the Envato marketplace where I sell some of my royalty- free music, and along with a few others like Pond5 (pond5.com), LuckStock (luckstock.com) and PremiumBeat (premiumbeat.com) are good examples of sites for passive earning. Once you've created a digital product it can be replicated infinitely and sold multiple times with little or no cost to you, yet you receive payment each time it is sold.

Other products that are ideal for passive earning include:

Graphics / illustrations
Digital photos
Website templates
Bits of code to stick in your website
Stock video footage
Video animations
Music
eBooks
Online training courses and tutorials
Online services like accounting software
Financial reports
Computer games
Phone apps

And the list goes on. If there's a demand for it, you can usually sell it!

The idea of a 'set and forget' income is what attracted and led Matt Harris, a talented composer, to give up his regular freelance design work and history of office jobs to push forward with a multi-stream lifestyle earning from his music. Known as *AlumoAudio* to his online peers, Harris says: 'Even though I was working for myself, I didn't like that. It didn't feel natural, it didn't make me feel particularly happy, which is of course why I've ended up in the stock music because it's literally: produce one item, let it out into the wild and the rest is magic. It works for itself. The product you produce works for itself rather than you working for somebody's expectation.'

He has had a lot of success online since starting to sell his music and earned a spot in the top-sellers of AudioJungle, interviewed by various websites, had regular features on other stock music sites, and his videos featured on YouTube.

Identifying skills to make them pay

Multi-stream earning is ultimately about finding or creating work that *enriches* your life and even the lives of others around you. It is a more holistic way of building activities into your life that support you financially, emotionally and satisfy your soul.

And although you might choose to work less and take more holidays in the end, I believe that you can build a lifestyle whereby the work you do slots into your life in a sustainable and enjoyable way. Multi-stream earning will give you a new perspective on what work is, allow you to break away from the conventional and outdated work model many of us follow and give you the freedom to weave the things you are passionate about into your life.

4

YOUR INNERPRENEUR

The first thing you need to do if you want to become a Lifestyle Entrepreneur is locate your inner entrepreneur. And no, that is not New Age talk in 21st century guise delivering the message that becoming an entrepreneur means connecting to some mystical you, a spiritual force guiding your being.

What I have in mind is taking the time to think long and hard about which of those skills, talents, passions and hobbies that we have already talked about come to the fore as something you can imagine devoting your thoughts, mental and possibly physical energy to, as well as enthusiasm and dynamism. In other words, find the means to take the important first steps towards becoming a fully-fledged Lifestyle Entrepreneur.

One of the things that makes this idea particularly daunting is that our education is so thoroughly geared towards learning subjects in a particular way and with a particular focus. Few children are taught at an early age how they might be able to survive by their own imagination and skills. The idea that we all have it in us to be an entrepreneur only seems to come on stream at the time schoolchildren are thinking of careers, and then more often than not, the emphasis will be on shaping your ideas to fit the requirement of an established business.

As mentioned earlier, the idea that if you study hard, go to university and get good marks you will get a job is turning out to be far less reliable than it once was. All the while, young people have not been encouraged at all to be enterprising, individualistic or to follow their passions and hobbies as a way to create the work they want. To work in a way that might contribute to a better world. Yet all these are possible as a LE as we shall see.

The rich-equals-happy delusion

In the early years of my working life, being a company executive, a banker, or a lawyer, where status comes with high earnings, was what marked you as a career success story. Not having thrusting ambition and the desire to gain riches and a high profile, with the possibility that one day your name might be up there in gilded figures on the *Sunday Times Rich List*, was to be a loser, someone who didn't fit the ethos of the times.

But it appears to me there has been a significant shift in that value system in the past few years. Many of my generation have seen the dark side of what a full-throttle, high earning life means in terms of lifestyle, relationships and having a space for personal development. And scientific research has been coming out with some pretty depressing findings on the hidden cost of a work life that seems to offer a guarantee of the Good Life, but in fact does not.

Just to give you a thumbnail sketch: Kate Pickett and Richard G. Wilkinson, in their book *The Spirit Level: Why More Equal Societies Almost Always Do Better*, were forerunners with an international comparative research study demonstrating that the greater wealth inequality in a developed country, the greater people's discontent and unhappiness. This was followed up by psychologists, philosophers and scientists using different measures to demonstrate how working extensive hours under great pressure can all too easily leave you profoundly exhausted and depressed.

Psychotherapist Andrew Mitchell has written in-depth about the breakdown of families where the man, and increasingly the woman, works at a pitch that requires every ounce of their energy, will usually travel often and find it difficult to relax when there is time. There may be scant physical time to spend as family and usually less emotional energy.

Even more daunting, because it is unseen forces at work, are the constant rushes of adrenaline when, say an all important deal is being done. The low that comes if it fails, the hormones called on hour after hour, day after day of working under stress and possibly for a relentless superior. John Coates describes vividly in his intriguing book, *The Hour Between Dog and Wolf: Risk-taking, Gut Feelings and the Biology of Boom and Bust*, how this pattern is profoundly detrimental to one's health, and may dramatically alter how our personality manifests.

And that is just for starters. So it is a mighty positive outcome, in my view, that fashion is swinging from the over-riding ambition of getting a job with a company adored by the FTSE, with the steps to the top tantalisingly shown to you from day one, to becoming an innovative entrepreneur creating a work style that enables the life you want.

Finding your innerpreneur

As this chapter is dedicated to helping you identify your inner entrepreneur, I have not related it to multi-stream earning. Many people will begin with just one work stream as they learn how to operate as an entrepreneur, and the basic approach is the same whether it is applied to creating a single or several income streams. We are talking personal chutzpah here.

The most newsworthy of the new entrepreneurs tend to be young, and there is logic in this. If youthful generations can be a successful driving force creating sustainable businesses which will grow and possibly employ others - and some I hear about have started businesses soon after puberty, for goodness sake - then they may well play their part in shaping a new, exciting economy.

Frivolous inspiration

I couldn't help thinking how gloriously frivolous the impetus to become entrepreneurs sounds when you listen in to Viviane Jaeger and Emma-Jayne Parkes, Co-Founders of SquidLondon, which produces Squidarellas (umbrellas) that change colour as soon as the rain hits the panels, creating the ultimate walking piece of art: 'We thought it would be so cool to walk down the street, it starts to rain and your clothes turn into a walking Jackson Pollock.'

But by the time they had got serious and founded the business in 2008, the pair had spent time formulating a thoroughly thought out project whilst studying a four-year Product Design and Development degree at London College of Fashion, which culminated in their creating a business plan for the Deutsche Bank Award in their final year at University. They were helped a good deal by both having worked up to 80 hours a week for busy and demanding directors in fashion houses such as Chloe and Selina Blow during a placement year.

Their first stockist was Tate, commissioning them for the 'Paint Drip' Squidarella for the colour chart exhibition. Since then they have worked with the top leaders in the industry such as the British Museum, Colette, the Conran Shops, MoMA in NYC and Japan, and are stocked in 18 countries worldwide. For the London Olympics they were part of the LCF team designing the dance costumes and they also launched an exclusive London Olympics Squidarella for Accessorize. Viviane and Emma-Jayne have won many awards including the ERDF 'Most innovative business in London' Award 2012 and the Lloyds TSB Creative Enterprise Winner 2010.

There was a provocative article in the magazine of the LSE (London School of Economics) in which the authors asked: 'What makes a successful entrepreneur?'. It comes as no surprise that such traits as a high IQ, lots of education, abundant self-esteem and wealthy parents all contribute. But on the other side a recent report also found that smart teenagers who engage in illicit activities are more likely to become successful entrepreneurs than equally intelligent, rule-abiding teenagers. And in-between these categories are the more ordinary mortals like myself who can use our smarts to be sustainable Lifestyle Entrepreneurs despite liking to think of myself as a bit more edgy than I really am.

In other words there is no identikit type who has it in her or him to be an entrepreneur. It is about drive, planning, conviction, believing in yourself, your idea and having the get-up-and-go to make it happen.

Chocolate to Go

Sophi Tranchell used the strong sense of justice that took her over when she was working in the anti-apartheid movement with a background in campaigning to design a plan to make *Divine Chocolate*, produced by an African co-operative of farmers, a known and popular brand in the UK.

The co-operative, Kuapa Kokoo, producing *Divine Chocolate*, had placed an advertisement in the British press looking for a boss to lead the new company. They had been funded with investment from *Christian Aid*, *The Body Shop* and *Comic Relief*, as well as being given a loan to help them secure bank finance to set up in the UK by the British Government.

Sophi had no experience in retail or the chocolate business - she had been running a film distribution business - but she convinced those interviewing her that she had the passion and persistence it would need to set up this innovative UK enterprise. It took dogged work, but she got the *Divine Chocolate* bars into UK supermarkets - *Sainsbury's* agreed to stock *Divine Chocolate's* first products at its stores and she devised a plan to get the bars into stores nationwide.

Sophi can smile now when she recalls: 'People said the company wouldn't work.' As Managing Director of Divine she has received an MBE, the Good Deals Pioneer Award for social enterprise leaders, and she is Chair of *Fairtrade London* and a *London Food Board* member.

The idea for your enterprise

Quite understandably, many of us carry in our heads the belief that an idea which can be turned into a sustainable way of earning will take long hours of thinking and working out, and that it may be painfully elusive. Or that it should arrive like one of those big bubbles above the head in cartoons, giving instructions.

In fact some of the most successful and rewarding ideas can be the result of just ten minutes shooting the breeze with a friend, a concept that has been lurking in the back of your mind suddenly shaping up, or a phone call that lets you know the idea you have is feasible. Or it can be, as it was for me, the result of a few spare minutes when I surfed the net and came across the online platform Fiverr, which features a very large marketplace of people offering services that start at five dollars.

I saw they had a popular section featuring voice-over recordings and, as I'd been told by a friend that my voice sounded 'radio-friendly' one day during a conversation, I decided to try it out. Being a bit of a clown - my parents still giggle remembering the spoof characters I adopted as persona during family holidays - I spared an hour of my time to do a demo recording. The result was an exaggerated colonial English accent and I applied some sound effects to so it sounded like a vintage BBC recording, something you would expect to be played out of a radio in the 1950's (or find in a Monty Python sketch).

I uploaded my demo to my profile page, which costs nothing as you pay a small percentage of anything you earn to Fiverr, and got on with the other work I had to do. I certainly wasn't waiting with bated breath for results. I had done it for fun and because I like sowing seeds of all kinds to see if some opportunities may come up. But within a day or two, I'd had an order, then another and another, until I realised I'd earned around $100 in a month. I was recording all sorts of scripts, from a 1950's-style World Cup film for a Brazilian client who was reporting on the World Cup at the time, to impersonating an old Colonel for an Indian play, and doing a comedy podcast about the danger of clowns and what to do when you see one.

Since then, I've added another gig for more professional voice-over work (in a normal accent!), which has brought in a steady stream of work. I've become a top-rated seller as a result and have gone from making around $100 a month to over $2,000.

An idea born over coffee and a chat

Barbara Gunnell, in her 60s, explains how the idea for a free university came up over a cup of coffee with Jonny Mundey and Martin Bright, a former journalist colleague from the Observer. They had been working together on a project for NEETS (Not In Education, Employment of Training) just as the Government's plans for 'screwing young people further with higher tuition fees was getting underway. I proposed that we find the expertise among colleagues and friends to get programmes of free seminars and lectures going and to help young people find free cultural resources around London. But it was Jonny's enthusiasm and elaborations that gave the project legs.'

Both were multi-stream earners, Barbara as a journalist, researcher and editor, and Jonny, in his 20s, was earning from different sources. He had founded the Office of Cultural Construction, an independent cultural consultancy based in London and when you open the website it comes up with a glorious visual saying simply 'Bon Nuit Ennui'.

'I had read cultural history at Manchester to Masters level; I was working on digital commissions for the think tank of the British Council, and gaining significant experience in the third sector, working with the arts employment charity The Creative Society and with clients such as The Royal Opera House, BFI and Google. And earning from writing for different organisations and some web design.'

He was also playing in a band doing gigs and is now in three 'that I think have potential in different ways.' At the time he was anxious about making a living from what he was doing and 'I was putting a lot of emphasis on finding a part-time 3-day-a-week stable job to complement my creative work. Interestingly, this came along, in the form of a 6-month part-time freelance contract with my old employer. However, by the time this was ending I realised it wasn't necessarily the project-based nature of the multistream that was the problem but that the work - simple web design - wasn't playing to my strengths.

You might imagine that being part of a benighted generation that had no jobs, poor pension prospects and work security as rare as hen's teeth, I would have jumped at the offer of a permanent part-time job at my old employer. But I didn't. By this time the Lifestyle Entrepreneur way was too much part of how I wanted things to be.'

Barbara explains how they went on to make IF viable: 'I carried on doing one strand of my work and diverted the earnings to the project. It had to be free. The whole point was that this education was - in Jonny's words - free at the point of delivery. Getting a summer school going was harder work than I had imagined and immensely stressful. We had good support from friends and a couple of people wrote articles about the plan, which upped our public profile.

'People either got the idea and loved it or thought it was bit hippyish. But we now have around us terrific professors willing to teach for nothing, lovely postgraduates who we do pay because they are part of this squeezed generation too. The summer school students were just terrific - so different from us. They were habitually late which had me tearing my hair out; hardly drank or smoked; a few held down jobs and even managed to socialise as well. They would in my day have gone straight from A-level to university. These had to think twice about it.

'Now we need to raise some financial support. (We had one successful crowdfunding effort). It may be free at the point of delivery and we may have loads of offers of help. But rooms have to be paid for. Administration has to be done and copies of *The Odyssey* have to be bought. I'm not sure what would count as success. Loads of people copying the idea, I think. And enough income to run two or three courses a year for a bit.'

A life-threatening illness

The people in this chapter have taken a shot at unusual ideas that excited them enough to put in a prodigious amount of energy, and they now see a sustainable way ahead for them. Not all are making big money. Indeed in some cases there is very little money as they attempt to build, or because they choose to work on social enterprise projects where profits go back into the enterprise or are used for community good. Or perhaps they have chosen a lifestyle where living modestly is preferable to working too many hours.

It took a life-threatening illness to get Alex Norton's inner entrepreneur to take a leap from working on something that might work sometime, to dynamic action.

Alex, 29, is another who sees his paid job as a graphic artist as a valuable support system while he develops a project he hopes will become part of a multi-stream way of earning. Inspiration came from his father, who 'instead of reading bedtime stories would sit me down in a beanbag next to the computer and he'd load up games like Might and Magic, Stonekeep, and we would play together. We would live the stories together.'

So even as a child his head was full of invented intricate playground games and from here he began building games systems: 'I was influenced by Dungeons and Dragons and Choose Your Own Adventure Books. At university I learnt to write video games of my own and I had a breakthrough where I found a way to create a game world that would 'make itself'. I saved the code and it sat there for many years.'

That might have been the end of it but for a sudden, life-threatening illness he contracted just after marrying. 'The doctors thought I would not make it but thanks to the talents of a gifted surgeon and my lovely wife Nyssa who was a rock throughout, I survived.'

But before that, 'a huge paradigm shift took place and when I was going in for surgery from which I was unlikely to wake, I had the realisation that if I didn't make it, nothing of "me" would be left behind. So when I did wake up I vowed to make a game that would last forever. I remembered the technology I had developed years earlier and the concept for *Malevolence: The Sword of Ahkranox*. I began immediately working on it in my evenings and at weekends. And once I was confident it really was a never-ending game I sought funding through Kickstarter and was able to make my game viable.'

Going solo at mid-life

Quitting a successful career, built up over years, to find out what you want to do next is something many people dream of, even fantasise about, at mid-life but few actually make a leap into the dark as 55-year-old Miriam Lahage did.

Miriam is a spirited, charming woman with a solid background working as vice president of a £20 billion organisation, but once her son finished university she gave up being a waged employee to 'see what I would do with my life.' It was a long shot. She had no plan of action and it still takes her by surprise to realise that the ad hoc business consultations she was offering to start-up entrepreneurs, as an add-on to her employed work, has turned into her own thriving enterprise through which she works with a diverse range of companies offering different kinds of guidance and advice. She has won a reputation as the go-to person for start-up entrepreneurs.

So how did her enterprise take root? 'An investor company approached me to see if I might be interested in doing a bit of consulting; the vice chairman of a business asked if I would be willing to come for a chat to see if we might do some work together. This happened over and over and now I have far more approaches than I can handle. But if I can't pursue them I give some advice and that is also a way of expanding my network.

'The exciting thing is to find that, at an age when people are talking retirement, I am on a new learning curve and having to keep myself well up to speed for so long as I want to do this.'

So here she is now giving strategic guidance to an online fashion site run by two school friends who have won the online shops for the *Daily Telegraph* and the *Evening Standard*. There is a premium plus fashion company and the day we spoke she was spinning off to take part in a promotional film for them. There is a simulation software company who have bought her services, but she makes plain it is business not specialist expertise they buy: 'I am not an expert but I know how to build a business and I understand organisational development. I was drawn to this because they are brilliant founders, they have great technology.'

Socialpreneurs

Being the kind of entrepreneur who taps into business ideas that attract clients who make it possible to build a decent profit base, a good salary for yourself, and any employees you may take on, is one way. But encouragingly I see plenty of my peers concerned enough about a society that is run so thoroughly on a capitalist model, built on making big bucks for those prepared to sell their lives and sometimes souls to this end, to want to direct their inner entrepreneurs to social enterprise.

So nowadays, almost like an alternative life support system, entrepreneurs who want to do something that feels worthwhile, are setting up an ever-growing range of non-profit-making projects, which often scarcely pay a living wage to the entrepreneur who has made it happen. But the pay off, and I have heard it said over and over, is the pleasure in doing something where the social benefits are very clear and where it may be doing its part to show how this can be every bit as rewarding and life-enhancing as seeing your annual salary make the living wage look like a handful of small change.

On your bike

Andrew Denham started *The Bicycle Academy* in 2011 with the aim of 'making frame-building more accessible' and if possible to do so in a way that would benefit others in need. He tells his story:

'Before starting the Bicycle Academy I had either volunteered or raised money for a few different charities that provide people in Africa with bicycles, so offering to support these charities by providing bicycle frames seemed like a great idea and it was very well received. I came up with the 'Make a bike. Make a difference.' idea: a course where people learn how to build a bicycle frame, keep the skills and give their first bike to someone who really needs it.

'I based the TBA Africa bike on the Buffalo Bike, which is designed specifically for people in Africa. It's the most widely distributed bike in Africa so I made sure that the TBA bike uses all of the same standardised components. It's tough, and thanks to the fantastic standard components it uses it can last for five years without much maintenance. The tyres are puncture-resistant - good for travelling over rugged ground. The design is simple, so it's easy to look after and it doesn't need lots of fiddly parts if anything does go wrong. It's strong, so it can carry heavy loads. And it's flexible, so it can be used for all kinds of different things like going to school or work, collecting food and water, helping health workers get from A to B, and even as an ambulance.'

'We opened our doors in July 2012 and so far more than 150 high quality, purpose built, steel 'Africa Bike' frames have been made thanks to help and support of every 'Africa Bike' course student and all of our crowdfunding backers. It's taken a tremendous amount of work to get this far, but it's been very worthwhile and each of our students have developed many wonderful skills along the way.'

'So far we've covered the cost of all materials used to make all of the frames and forks, and we're pleased to say that we have now secured transportation of the frames from the UK to Africa. In the meantime the frames are being stored here at *The Bicycle Academy* in a big rack ready to undergo the next stages of their journey towards being given to people in need.'

'We are fully supportive of each of the charities that have been linked to this project at different times and greatly admire the fantastic work that they do. Our original plan was to work with a charity that would ship and assemble the frames into ready-to-ride bicycles. We've secured a source for the components; a charity that's based in Africa that will supply them at their cost price, but what we are yet to find is an organisation or charity that can fund the purchase of these components, so we'd love to hear from you if you can help us to do so. Finding willing recipients for the bikes is straightforward, as many projects have expressed a real interest in taking the bikes. Completing and delivering the bikes to those most in need is a big logistical challenge, but one which we have always been and remain completely committed to.'

Bringing together the homeless and landlords

Katharine Hibbert set up DotDotDot, a social enterprise that works with landlords to protect their void properties by letting people who do amazing voluntary work live in them really cheaply as property guardians.

The idea came from what she learned researching Britain's wasted housing for her first book, *FREE: Adventures on the Margins of a Wasteful Society*. 'This took nearly 2 years because the book was about living for free, and about what happens when you opt out of normal working and spending patterns.

'Having written the book, I really became very bothered about the number of empty homes that there are and the problems that they cause, and I felt that I had enough knowledge, and enough ideas, to do something practical about it.'

Katharine is director of DotDotDot but she knew a good idea was only the first step. To get it off the ground, she knew that a coherent idea, and a business plan that fits around that - as in, what does the service actually look like, who are the competitors, what does it cost, what are the risks, how do you manage the risks, what's the insurance, what are the legal contracts - were essential. And, 'because of my working style, the thing that I felt the most need for was a network of other people to work with on it. So that was an advisory board of people who were relevant and expert.'

She began working on the idea with friend Emily Perkin, who has a background in management consultancy and who worked on it for one day a week: 'then we were really fortunate to get some funding in Autumn 2011, so we were already doing a bit of work, but up to that point we hadn't been paid anything from DDD. I was making money from other things like journalism.'

There had been cash investment that Katharine and Emily between them put into DDD, which came to about £2,500 - mostly insurance and legal fees. 'Obviously that's a lot of money but I could earn it from other sources.' She was working then, like now, as a freelance journalist for one of her work streams.

They also had the 'great good fortune' to get £15,000 from a charity called the Bromley by Bow Centre, which supports social enterprises. Katharine considers: 'I think we could have done without that, but it would have been a bit more painful, because the money meant that Emily and I could start being paid the minimum wage for the work that we were doing, and also gave us a bit more credibility and some more connections which was really helpful.'

They have received grants from the cabinet office, via Nesta, through their innovation and giving programme. 'This has been brilliant, but that has been money that has made it safer and easier for us to scale up, rather than to pay for the day to day running of the existing business. It's helped increase capacity - so that's money we'd have otherwise have had to get from equity investors or from loans. We haven't needed these.' The rest of the turnover is from money coming in and going out from landlords and guardians.

The success of DotDotDot comes from the enthusiasm of landlords for the project, which has their properties looked after well and by guardians who are not tenants but licensees, so can be asked to move at very short notice if necessary. While Katharine is clear that she is offering a service a cut above most: 'standards in the property guardian world are not that high - so we're better to deal with.' While from the point of view of guardians, 'the nature of the property system means that anyone in their right mind wants to live somewhere for less than £300 a month in central London. The deal is, in return for cheap living, the guardians are expected to do around 20 hours a week volunteering at something that does good for their community.'

Making a social enterprise financially viable and dynamic is a hard process. Katharine explains their approach: 'we are committed to not paying dividends for at least the next year (to the end of 2015), and after that we'll make a decision about the relationship between the profits and the business model, because obviously that's a bit complicated as a social enterprise. We more than cover our costs by trading and the surplus gets reinvested.'

Their costs include the eight staff they now have, including Katharine, and their London office. A substantial cost is risk mitigation, 'which is expensive: insurance, contingency funds, professional standards, legal costs.'

DotDotDot is the big job, but Kate combines this with work as a freelance journalist for national newspapers including *The Sunday Times* and *The Guardian*, and for *The Pavement*, a magazine for homeless people. She adds to this being a consultant on waste and empty homes and is a trustee of Headway East London, a charity that supports survivors of brain injury.

Just try it out

Tapping into your inner entrepreneur needn't be a long-drawn out process and, in fact, it's probably better to have a few ideas to try out at a time so you can test what really captures your interest and shows potential. As my experiment with voice-over work demonstrated, even frivolous little ideas can quickly turn into something much bigger, particularly if there's strong demand for what you're offering. All it takes is a little time, initiative and commitment.

5

CAN I LEARN TO BE AN ENTREPRENEUR?

Right now I can hear you saying, as you finish the chapter before this, all good stuff but how do I know whether I have an inner entrepreneur lurking there, ready to provide the engine to drive my idea to the point where it becomes a viable enterprise? How do I know what an entrepreneur is supposed to feel like? To think like? How do I know if the way I conceptualise an idea is on the right lines to convert it into an earning stream? And even when I think I really have identified a go-er and the entrepreneurial sap has risen, how do I know what moves to make in approaching the marketplace effectively?

Can you learn to be an entrepreneur?

This is, of course, the million dollar question. Do some emerge into the world and quickly show their entrepreneurial skills like Becky John, founder of *Who Made Your Pants?* clearly did. At the age of eight she was popping into social events selling sweets and thinks she developed an entrepreneurial drive at that time. That, combined with a love of lingerie - she has long been 'a serial purchaser of gorgeous undies' - and a determination to do something for human rights, came together six years ago when she founded her own lingerie company *Who Made Your Pants?* which now employs, among others, refugee women in Southampton, many single parents. The name is a challenge as much as a gimmicky label.

Becky explains how she got involved in a film for the Open University about sweatshops which made her starkly aware and angry at the exploitation and cruelty so often involved in cheap manufacturing of clothing, so she started wondering where the lingerie she so loved actually came from. Who was making it?

That set her realising that while she might not be able, single-handedly, to change the way the cheap garment manufacturers operate, she could set up a business that would show a different way and help women who have had a hard time in life, and often have few opportunities to help themselves through education and work.

She raised funding to set up a little factory in Southampton where they buy in fabrics that big underwear companies would otherwise turn into waste at the end of the season and they employ refugee women who badly need to work and earn as well as having some stability.

Becky knew, however, when she set up *Who Made Your Pants?* that some of the women would not speak English, some might well need counselling and all would need training in the work of making the lingerie. 'I was able to do this, helped by my team, because the business wouldn't work if we couldn't give the women the care they need'.

In return the women work hard and with enthusiasm to create the best garments they can and, as Becky says, that is essential. 'We think it is also good for the women to have high standards expected of them. Some have been promoted to supervisor. They take pride in what they do and we pay them properly. We all live from what we earn.'

So it is very gratifying, Becky says, through a recession which has hit hard at the clothing business, to see sales climbing steadily: 'Last year we had 160 per cent of the last year's sales and all the profits go back into the business.'

Your Hidden Potential (YHP), a leading UK web publication with a focus on entrepreneurship, start-ups, growth and innovation, points out in 2013 over half a million new businesses were created (a record-breaking 526,446 as reported by Companies House), with almost a quarter of a million by halfway through

2014. And YHP take a view: 'What this demonstrates is that there has never been a better time when it comes to starting a business and it's no surprise considering the multitude of services available at your fingertips to help get you started, many of which are new businesses themselves!'

We hear similarly upbeat news from Nesta, (National Endowment for Science, Technology and the Arts) an independent charity set up to increase the innovation capacity of the UK through practical programmes, investment, policy, research and forming partnerships. They tell of an increasing investment in innovation which had reached £137.5bn in 2011.

Indeed, Amar Lodhia, CEO of the Small Business Consultancy, a social enterprise based in London, focuses on how young people with difficult backgrounds can turn into 'income-generating assets' for the economy, as he told *The Economist* magazine. So TSBC provides a powerful support programme with mentoring in an area of interest to help these so often disenfranchised young turn their anti-social behaviour and disruptiveness into becoming entrepreneurs.

Certainly there are a good number of people out there who believe they can teach how to be an entrepreneur and have devoted their careers to doing so. As your guide in this book, I have learned from some who have helped teach and inspire the founders of the hundreds of start-ups that have emerged from their courses.

If you want an optimistic eye on your chances, turn to Professor Nicos Nicolaou at Warwick Business School, who declares that he believes 'most people can become successful entrepreneurs given the right training, education, relevant industrial experience and advice.'

Entrepreneurship is not rocket science

His first aim was to demystify entrepreneurship so that it does not seem like some exotic talent that only a few have. 'I try to give my students the tools that will enable them to recognise and exploit an entrepreneurial opportunity.' And while he would not 'put them all in one basket' Professor Nicolaou believes most are characterised by:

A high need for achievement
A creative personality
High perceptive ability
Capable of learning the fundamentals of entrepreneurship

To get on the course you need to be an MBA student and to write a business plan, which will be assessed for viability, as your equivalent of an entrance exam. I thought the course sounded rigorous and interesting - almost made me want to be a student again! - with classes in evaluating an entrepreneurial opportunity, writing business plans, understanding venture capital finance, as well as crowd funding and evaluating ways in which firms can protect their intellectual property.

And that's just part of what Professor Nicolau believes can give students the best chance of making it on what he sees as a 'roller coaster ride'. That is so long as they avoid underestimating the competitive landscape and avoiding splitting equity, as he fears too many people do. He quips: 'There is a saying that equity is like manure, if you pile it up it smells bad, but if you spread it around lots of wonderful things grow....'

As we saw earlier, Suzanne Noble has pulled together projects working with graphic artists, creating sex videos, working for a soldier's charity and building her entertainment app Frugl. It was as she began this that she was accepted on to a course at the Accelerator Academy run by the 'dynamic and inspiring Ian Merricks.' It helped her focus her mind, she says, on precisely what she wanted to achieve and how she was going to make it workable.

It was costing her £5,000 of her own money to launch and she wanted as much guidance and information on this particular style of entrepreneurship as she could get. And although she could criticise aspects of the course (and being an analytical woman with very clear views, she does), overall, it was a thumbs up Suzanne says, and eighteen months after its launch, Frugl was a very active app.

Digital dynamism

Digital start-ups is one thing they specialise in at the Accelerator Academy and, I learned, they are keen to work with businesses that have more than one person, although they don't rule out singles. I was intrigued by Merrick's thinking here and I could see how doing a course where they treat you not as a student, but as someone who will need to raise funding, could be very helpful. Ian explains, 'if a person can't find a single other person to believe in their idea, then investors may not either. Investors are not enthusiastic about backing sole founders because they see it as too risky.'

This is a course that intends to put you on the path to setting up your own start up. It is 12 weeks, each of which is separately themed, and every student has a mentor for the whole time. During midweek clinics they sit down with industry professionals, which seems to me a missed opportunity for many of us going it alone. It set me thinking that it would be a smart move for a group of Lifestyle Entrepreneurs working in the same line to approach an industry to see if someone would spare an hour or so of their time to give guidance and insights.

The course which, since it began in 2011, had worked with 74 start-ups, is kept to part-time so that wannabe entrepreneurs can have days free to build their businesses. There are three main things they try to impart, Merricks says. All the prospective businesses they oversee are digital and they cover many kinds of technology. And no, it's no casual ride, Merricks is clear:

'Over the past two years we have developed a 15-point selection criteria, published on our website. We don't wish to have "wantrepreneurs" who talk about it and never do it. Our students need to have a plan and to be working full-time on their business idea. We look for them to be experts in their area. It's not a field of dreams scenario where that is enough to get you there. I boil it down to them needing to be bright enough and humble enough.'

He pinpoints three things that students need to demonstrate as they go through the course:

- Team readiness: everyone in place with distinct roles to be sure people are focusing on exactly what they are meant to be doing.
- Market readiness - is the product being sold to the right customers at the right price? Do they need more market engagement?
- Investor readiness - are those looking for investment doing the right things? Can they demonstrate strong valuation for the business?

And those who have the right entrepreneurial spirit are certainly helped along their way, it appears. Of 70-odd start-ups supported by the Academy, 81% of the alumni have raised follow up funding - £12million in total - in two years. But Ian warns not all will survive and for this reason they are cautious about who they take on the course: 'It's become so trendy to want to be an entrepreneur, but what people need to realise is that getting the skills marketable is a tough challenge.'

The importance of today's new entrepreneurs understanding digital technology lies behind the creation of the BBC Worldwide Labs. These were set up to promote and showcase emerging digital media and technology companies within the UK. For a six month programme they select six start-ups to join the programme and integrate them into the BBC infrastructure, which includes office space at BBC Worldwide and mentoring by internal and external industry experts. 'Our goal', they explain, 'is to strategically and commercially partner with and support the most innovative up-and-coming digital media companies that are helping to define the emerging digital landscape'.

The Target Age: 20 - 27 Years
It can be daunting when you are striving to find a way to skill up and start up earning streams to hear such grand statements, but

there are certainly less grandiose sounding places to turn for help. As Neeta Patel explains: 'The New Entrepreneurs Foundation (newentrepreneursfoundation.com) recognises that the job market is not offering many talented young people as good opportunities as they may be able to create for themselves. So, the organisation is targeting young people age 20 - 27 - the generation snapping at my ankles - offering them an alternative training to the traditional graduate scheme which takes people at the end of a degree course and trains them up to work in a firm.'

'We want to create the next generation of entrepreneurs. We're looking for passion, we're looking for people who are really driven, single-minded and good communicators. We need to see skill as leaders but also team players.'

If anyone has seen the growing trend to become a Lifestyle Entrepreneur, where aiming for fame and fortune is less the idea than wanting a balanced life and with the wish to do lots of different things, it is the younger generation. They want to know how to make this goal work for them.

I am well aware of what opportunities technology has opened up and that my own way of working is very dependent on the online world. At NEF they recognise and work with this. Neeta considers: 'technology has created a whole new series of businesses that even ten years ago couldn't have existed. And I think there's more funding available at an earlier stage'.

But have no illusions it is an easy ride. 'We say to students that entrepreneurship actually isn't something you can do while you're doing something else. Because it's a sort of 16 hours a day, 7 days a week commitment...If you speak to any successful entrepreneurs they'll say they didn't have a holiday for 10 years [and] they need to be resilient - because they're going to fail, at some point.'

It might have been difficult during the days when Gordon Geko (Michael Douglas in the film *Wall St*) smacked his lips, declaring greed is good, to imagine new generations wanting to involve themselves in working for the good of others and the community. But they existed then and have become part of the important way that Lifestyle Entrepreneurs are changing the landscape of what satisfying work looks like.

School for entrepreneurs to help community

The School for Entrepreneurs Dartington, in the belly of the verdant rolling Devon countryside, was started with precisely this kind of socially conscious mindset at its heart by Michael Young, a prolific entrepreneur and social innovator, who launched over forty organisations during his career including the Open University, *Which?* Magazine, and the Consumers Association.

At the School there is training and opportunities that enable people with entrepreneurial ideas to achieve positive change in their communities. The approach is centred on you and your project. Tutors help shape the learning opportunities according to the visions and needs of the people who come because they are committed to making a difference within their communities and in their society: people whose objectives are about more than profit. Expect a different kind of pedagogy here. They say, 'our learning process is powered by action and reflection and is far removed from the traditional educational and learning programmes.'

Disabled entrepreneurs

Like almost everyone I know, fortunate enough to be able-bodied and healthy, I rarely stop to wonder how it would be building a business if you had an impairing disability. But I was alerted to thinking about the increased level of enterprise you need if you are disabled and want to create your own working life by an article in the *Guardian* newspaper. The starting point has to be answering the question, 'what can't I do?', as well as, 'what can I do?' and for someone with health issues and disabilities, a home setting can provide the freedom and flexibility they need to run a successful business.

Just how cruel the work environment can be if you are disabled was illuminated for me by the experience of Paul Nicol, who by age 28 was almost completely blind and was made redundant from his job as an IT support team manager. He knew working from home would make sense and the bonus is he can organise work time to suit him and his family.

He set up iCAN Experiences, a home-based business that specialises in providing gift experience activities, some as adventurous as sky-diving, with specialised helpers, and days out for people with a range of disabilities.

Disabled Entrepreneurs have a campaigning determination to improve opportunities for the disabled to work. They talk of 'providing a voice and networking opportunities for all disabled entrepreneurs in the UK,' and they particularly encourage disabled people running their own enterprises to contact them. For some truly inspiring stories of this type of entrepreneurship, take a look at their website (disabledentrepreneurs.co.uk). It is frankly humbling.

There is a very clear set of objectives, which are much broader than just offering training in entrepreneurship. They know well that self-employment can present some challenges and is not for every disabled person. But they also know that for many with disabilities and chronic health conditions, self-employment offers the hope of making a living and achieving self-sufficiency. So their mission is to inspire, to provide networking opportunities among disabled people of all ages and disabilities. And I like to think that those of us who may have the opportunity to work with or offer work to someone with a disability, will do so. After all if being a LE is about human values as well as just a different way to work, it makes sense.

Mark Esho

As a black disabled man trying to set up his company *Easy Internet Services* 10 years ago, Mark Esho is one inspiring story, and I ask you to pause for a moment to hear how tough it was for him. He had childhood polio and has difficulty walking any distance. So getting 'zero support' when he was trying to set up added to his feeling of being marginalised.

Mark says, 'It was a new technology and people didn't understand what I was trying to do in setting up SEO (Search Engine Optimisation). At the time there were only four of us in the UK doing SEO. I started my business on a credit card and I had to work for three months without pay while I built up my portfolio. It was pretty hard. If you are black and disabled you have two things going against you.'

Mark's interest in business came when he decided to do an MBA while drifting from job to job in London, as he explained to the *Leicester Mercury*. He then worked at city disabled charity *Mosaic* for a while before taking the plunge. Because of his polio Mark suffers from chronic fatigue two or three times a month so feels he is best suited to running his own business.

By persevering Mark has built success. *Easy Internet Services*, in Leicester, now employs 17 people and claims to have 50,000 customers. There is a turnover around the £1 million mark and such clients as the Co-op and The Guardian newspaper, with profits increasing by 10 to 15 per cent during the recession. He is winner of the Race Entrepreneur of Excellence 2012, National Diversity Awards.

The Virtuous Circle

In 2006, when he was 31 years old, Mark Pearson founded *Markco Media*, a global web- based marketing and advertising company. He has watched his business, which operates a run of voucher deal networks grow sales of £500 million in 2008 and offers advice to young entrepreneurs: 'Don't be afraid to ask for help; seek advice from others. Get your business on social networking platforms and engage with others in the industry. I learned a lot from peers.'

It is certainly one of the most effective ways for all entrepreneurs to help themselves, agrees Miriam Lahage, who uses social media a good deal to get to know people where an exchange of knowledge and contacts can be so valuable. It is the generosity of the online community I talked about earlier, and Miriam has a name for the process of helping each other as 'the virtuous circle.'

6

THE BUSINESS OF FUNDING

You have a great idea - couldn't fail, certain to make millions, you quip with your mates, or maybe you are burning to set up a social enterprise that will really make a difference, but, once the cheery spin is over there is the small matter of what will it cost? And where will money needed come from?

So let's think long and hard about this because money has a way of being uncomfortably elusive when you really want it. Some questions. Do you have money available to set up your project? Or might you at least need seed funding, some kind of base line money available as a means of survival for the first months? And if your idea involves serious overheads and equipment you will probably need serious finance. So what to do? Where to go?

Be well wised-up

Clearly it is a good idea to do all the homework you can if you are planning to borrow money. People's experiences range from the very contented to the disgusted and disillusioned. Do you know people who have financed projects? How has it worked for them? Can you get a recommendation for a good place to go? It is worth reading up the reports of financial journalists (if they are writing impartially) about the kind of loan you are considering. Make sure the questions you have to ask cover everything you need to know, if an investor offers to talk to you. And remember you are going to have to sell your idea and yourself effectively to get the money.

It is also worth keeping in mind the thoughts of Bryce

Courtenay author of *The Power of One* who would like us to imbibe his homegrown philosophy:

'The power of one is above all things the power to believe in yourself, often well beyond any latent ability you may have previously demonstrated. The mind is the athlete, the body is simply the means it uses to run faster or longer, jump higher, shoot straighter, kick better, swim harder, hit further, or box better.'

That's the conviction part, but you also need enough confidence in yourself to convince others, who don't know you from Adam or Eve, that they should put good money into bringing your idea to life.

Believe in me, fund me

There are various ways you might get funding. It could be help from family or friends enthused by your idea. You might decide to apply for one of the government's start up loans, secure funding as Katharine Hibbert, who started the social enterprise DotDotDot, did through Nesta. Or you could be among the lucky few and find an angel investor who, if you have a strong business idea, will discuss investment with you. You might decide to live dangerously, despite all the warnings, and use a credit card. Or you might try crowdfunding.

There is an unmistakably knowing note in what Drew Hendricks of the American financial magazine *Forbes* says:

'Have you ever asked for money? It's not exactly the highlight of your day. But that's nothing compared to applying for a loan or meeting with potential investors. It's one of the most nerve-wracking experiences that entrepreneurs have to go through.'

The hard sell business plan

However you choose to look for funding, you will need to have a business plan and a committed way of putting across why your project really deserves - no, needs - to be funded. Business writer Alan Gleeson (http://articles.bplans.co.uk/starting-a-business/five-reasons-you-need-a-business-plan) has thought this through:

'Without a plan, or using a cookie cutter business plan template, a business is essentially rudderless, and day-to-day activities are likely to be haphazard and reactive, in stark contrast to those businesses implementing a well thought out business plan.

'A business plan is not just required to secure funding at the start-up phase, but is a vital aid to help you manage your business more effectively. By committing your thoughts to paper, you can understand your business better and also chart specific courses of action that need to be taken to improve your business. A plan can detail alternative future scenarios and set specific objectives and goals along with the resources required to achieve these goals.

'By understanding your business and the market a little better and planning how best to operate within this environment, you will be well placed to ensure your long-term success.'

Paul Jones at technori.com approaches it with a simple logic that I find helpful. He says:

'I think the key to understanding why you need a business plan, is in understanding what a business plan for a startup is all about.'

But to really grasp the point Paul suggests starting with what a business plan is not about:

'A start up business plan is not an operating plan. It is not a cookbook for running the business. In the high impact entrepreneurship space, a business plan is better thought of as an investment plan, and it is written for potential investors. (But) the point is that no one—including even semi-competent potential investors—expects a startup's business will evolve as laid out in the first business plan.'

Yet he is clear that there are at least two cases to be made for creating a business plan: 'First, the process of creating a business plan—at least a credible one—demonstrates that the entrepreneur is capable of thinking about his or her idea in business and investment terms. That the entrepreneur can conceive of his or her baby, so to speak, as a tool rather than a child; as something that has to serve crass commercial and financial masters, as well as a prerequisite to serving any higher values. In twenty-five years in and around the venture capital business, I can assure you there are lots of entrepreneurs who can't or won't think of their baby in business/investor-centric terms.

'Beyond demonstrating this, a business plan provides a sanity check in that a good plan will demonstrate that there is at least one plausible way the entrepreneur's baby can be turned into a solid business and investment opportunity. Finding one plausible business model for a new idea is, in my mind, like finding life somewhere in the universe. Given how vast the universe is, if you find life in one place, it is bound to exist somewhere else. Similarly, if you can make at least one convincing business case for an idea, there are bound to be others out there.'

Hard-nosed approach

When the Wildcard Brewery team, who have gone from strength to strength, were looking to make their dream of running a brewery come to fruition they knew they had to be hard-nosed about it. Andrew tells:

'We had quite a strong idea of what we wanted to do and how we wanted to do it. We produced a detailed business plan and we put a lot of work into that because we needed to be absolutely clear our idea was viable. While writing a business plan you need to write down how many bottles you will sell to which customers in however many months. Unless you have done something like this before you will never be able to visualise what it is going to be like. So you need to be ready to change the plan whenever required.'

William adds, 'I would say you need to have a concrete plan on what you are going to do and three of us agreed, but you also have to accept that your understanding of the situation may change. Fortunately we know each other well enough to work through any times of crossed horns. We have all worked with people stuck with an idea about doing a thing and who would not change at any cost, and we knew that was not a workable way.

'You need to recognise the skills each brings: in our case we had level-headed Andrew, I am a good salesperson and Jaega brought her artistic ideas for packaging, posters, flyers, logo and all those important things.'

Ed Molyneux, founder of accountancy company FreeAgent, tells of the tough route to raising money for his business, which only happened two years after the launch.

'My co-founders Olly Headey and Roan Lavery and I bootstrapped the company for the first two years, working without pay and in our spare time. Luckily Olly and I were working on fairly well paid part-time freelancing contracts at the time, and Roan worked full-time in the day and worked on FreeAgent in the evenings, but the credit cards took a pretty serious battering back then. In 2009 we raised two rounds of seed funding to allow us to work full-time on the business.

'The first funding we secured in 2009 came from Christoph Janz, an angel investor based in Germany who was focused on companies building online tools for small businesses. Then, later in the year, we raised another small round from Robin Klein (The Accelerator Group) who has been ranked number 22 in *The Telegraph*'s most influential tech investors in Europe. Being able to dive into FreeAgent full-time meant it had the attention it needed to truly start to flourish.

'We have come a long way over the last six years – we now have more than 30,000 customers and have secured more than £4 million in external investment, and have strong partnerships with Barclays Bank and Iris Software.'

Crowdfunding

Crowdfunding has been the democratic funding revolution of the new millennium. It has opened the way to social enterprises, community projects, philanthropic initiatives, playful schemes, projects for sharing and caring that would have been very unlikely to see the light of day without this way of raising seed money, further development money, a budget to be stretched over a long production period and so on.

In the beginning

Crowdfunding, it is said, began in 1997 when fans underwrote the entire cost of a US tour for the British rock group Marillion, raising $60,000 through a fan-based Internet campaign. The group itself then went on to raise money to record and market such albums as *Anoraknophobia* and *Happiness is the Road*. The idea that money could be raised to produce music, such a notoriously difficult and expensive thing to do, caught on.

Electric Eel Shock, a Japanese rock band, became one of the first bands without a previous significant recording deal to embrace crowdfunding. As an unsigned band in 2004, they raised £10,000 from 100 fans who were offered a lifetime membership on the band's guest list.

The great virtue of crowdfunding is that it's available to anyone regardless of age, gender, class, race, or creed. Crowdfunding to my mind has been a brilliant development for today's young who have been hit by an ever-shrinking workplace, the dismal realisation that degrees and years of study do not guarantee a step on the career ladder and that idea many of us grew up with of a firm offering a job for life with a pension at the end, has become a unicorn. Nicole Fallon, at *Business News Daily* predicts that it can only grow and spread, going mainstream with a range of new trends emerging in the next decade with non-profits benefiting ever more and equity crowdfunding growing.

And when the mainstream financial industry takes crowdfunding seriously enough to put resources into examining the phenomenon, you know it is worth taking note. It is also worth hearing what they learn.

It is encouraging to hear someone like Drew Hendricks, who is plugged into the serious business of funding, say 'Compared to all of the paperwork and preparation needed for loans, setting a crowdfunding campaign is a breeze. Just select the right platform, put together a video and offer enticing rewards. While there's still a need for something that's important for the long-term, like a business plan, it's extremely refreshing to only have to make your presentation and pitch just once.

'Crowdfunding is also a great for both investors and entrepreneurs to discover each other. Instead of relying on traditional methods and investing options, crowdfunding provides a convenient and exciting way of obtaining an investment or finding a new venture to fund.'

Then there is the essential message to keep in mind at all times. Having an idea is one thing. Proving that the idea can make a profit is another thing. Whether you need to convince yourself or investors that there's money to be made, crowdfunding provides a great opportunity to see where the market stands. Back to Drew: 'If you launch a successful crowdfunding campaign, it not only proves that there's an interest in your idea, it also shows that people are willing to spend money on it. That's a rather effective way in validating your concept.'

Reducing risk

Because crowdfunding validates the market, neither entrepreneurs nor investors have to worry about taking on as much risk. Instead of dumping your savings into a business venture that doesn't have a sustainable market, you can test the water without much of an investment. In fact, even if your campaign isn't successful, the money that was given is often returned to all donors.

'Crowdfunding is also great for both investors and entrepreneurs to discover each other. Instead of relying on traditional methods and investing options, crowdfunding provides companies through all stages from seed to pre-IPO (an Initial Public Offering is the first time a company publicly sells shares on the market) and when listed. We do this through equity funding a convenient and exciting way of obtaining an investment or finding a new venture to fund,' says Drew Hendricks on Forbes.com.

Whether you need to convince yourself or investors that there's money to be made, crowdfunding provides a great opportunity to see where the market stands. At Fundable, where they support the crowdfunding approach, Will Schroter says:

'We enable both equity and crowdfunding and rewards crowd-funding. We've just completed a survey of the past year (in the US) to understand exactly why crowdfunding websites work so well. Our survey of successful campaigns has uncovered one very clear fact - crowdfunding is marketing, plain and simple. There's now a crowdfunding site for just about everything from yoga studios to medical devices.' (www.fundable.com)

At the funding platform Crowd for Angels (crowdfor-angels.com), the goal is to bring innovative and appealing products and provide funding for companies through their growth cycle. They support public and private UK companies through all stages from seed and do so through equity funding and debt funding through convertible loans, loans with warrants and other types of loans.

Their investors get the opportunity to connect, capitalise and share the growth prospects of small private or public companies at no cost to themselves. Companies only pay if the funding is a success.

There are now a great many crowdfunding platforms and often they have a specific focus from businesses aiming for large profits, and offering equity in return for crowdfund donations to those funding social enterprises because they believe in them. Kickstarter was the first, launched in the US and now over here.

Kickstarter

When Kickstarter was launched *Time* magazine described it as The 'Best invention of 2010'. The vital significance is that it has opened up the possibility of raising money for a start up way beyond the usual, conventional styles of funding for individual enterprises.

Kickstarter describes itself as for creative projects - not businesses per se - but the concept of crowdfunding has spread so that while some funders remain fairly open-ended about what you may raise money for, others specify that they are for the arts, social enterprise, or good causes such as GiveForward.com. Indiegogo and Buzzbnk are where people solicit funds for an idea, charity or start-up business.

FundaGeek is a crowdfunding resource for projects involving technology, scientific research, inventions and community support. EquityNet is a U.S.-based crowdfunding platform for startups and mature businesses to raise equity capital from accredited investors. Moola Hoop helps women fund their enterprises. Other crowdfunding sites such as Seedrs.com and Crowdcube.com are about getting investors for start ups.

Barbara Gunnell and Jonny Mundey were recommended to go to the well-established Kickstarter to raise funding for IF - a free university and innovative project offering free humanities courses to young people priced out of today's higher education market. As Jonny explains:

'London is awash with great culture - museums, free lectures, art galleries, concerts. The Internet is bursting with free lectures from the best thinkers of today. Loads of academics want to share their knowledge with a wider audience. Could we use these plentiful cultural resources to create an exciting learning experience - a high quality humanities course at no cost to the student?'

Barbara adds, 'It's stressful because you have to keep thinking of ways to get people to read the site and contribute…if you have good networks e.g. past readers of yours etc., publishing contacts, you will do well. Go for the lowest you can manage because if you don't reach your target you get nothing…and if you overshoot you get to keep the extra money.'

However, it can be a lucrative way to fund your project if you hit the zeitgeist. Being an 80's boy, a Kickstarter project which particularly caught my attention, launched back in December 2013, is Kung Fury, which raised $630,000 during its campaign. Described as 'an over-the-top action comedy' by Swedish writer / director David Sandberg, 'the movie features: arcade-robots, dinosaurs, Nazis, vikings, Norse gods, mutants and a super kung fu-cop called Kung Fury, all wrapped up in an 80s style action packed adventure.' (www.kungfury.com). Sandberg clearly hit the right market helped by the fact he tapped into the Synthwave (a popular musical genre) crowd who were chomping at the bit for this kind of production.

How does crowdfunding work?

The idea is simple. An online site is set up where people with an idea they need to fund explain what they are doing, why it is worth funding and the donations they need to give it legs. The appeal for many donors is that they can help an enterprising young entrepreneur, a project they see as benefiting the community, a scheme that may just hit the big time and which they can get to have a stake in.

And crowdfunders may well be given a reward in proportion to the amount donated from a DVD of a film, they may be credited as having helped to make the project work, free gifts, and sometimes equity in the business. The organisation that compiled a global report on crowdfunding (crowdsourcing.org) found that internationally crowdfunding had raised $6.1 billion by 2014 and its importance in helping entrepreneurs was noted.

Uniting crowdfunders

Alex Feldman set up the CrowdsUnite website as a place where people can get a great deal of information about crowdfunding. I like the way he describes this manner of raising money as cutting out the middleman (the bank) and allowing people to directly invest in the projects they choose. This way, investors can choose exactly how they invest their money and how they are rewarded.

But quite clearly for small scale entrepreneurs having a go at making a living with their own ideas, Feldman's point is that crowdfunding gives many small projects that would otherwise go unfunded to have the chance to receive the funding they need.

This said, he also suggests you think hard about whether crowdfunding is really right for you. It may sound like a bit of a lark, putting an idea out there and waiting for the donations to roll in, but in truth it is far more labour-intensive, Feldman warns:

'Crowdfunding requires a lot of work and more preparation than simply launching a campaign on a site. You must plan out a way of inviting a crowd to your page and how to encourage them to invest money. If you don't have a good network to reach out to, crowdfunding may not be for you. It's best not to think of crowdfunding as selling your product or idea, but actually selling a story to people that makes them feel good about investing money.'

Not commercial enough

Producer Kate Cook and Bruce Goodison had a tough time getting the funding they needed. They started out aware that an issue-based film like *Leave to Remain* - about unaccompanied minors who were seeking asylum in the UK - would need a community of support behind it, and that the best way to engage an audience early on would be to involve them in the process of getting it made.

Kate explains: 'We'd exhausted all traditional film funding options on the basis that the film wasn't commercial enough. We were interested in telling a story that didn't feel like it had been explored and one that very few people knew about, so crowdfunding was a way of doing this independently.'

They were, on the other hand, very aware of the pitfalls of crowdfunding based on an earlier experience, when it had been a massive administrative task to manage an enormous body of investors.

'Based on this experience', Kate continues, 'we decided to use an existing platform, which would take away a lot of the administration and also offer a portal for finding a further audience.'

They decided to work with a startup crowdfunding platform called Buzzbnk, geared towards people who wanted to support enterprising projects with a good cause at their heart. At this time *Leave to Remain* was the only film-related project.

'We created a project page and launched the campaign, advertising it to our existing network and inviting them to share with others, the expectation being that a new audience would also discover the project through Buzzbnk's own advertising network.'

They knew they had to set a target to reach and agreed on £45,000, which was comparatively high for a crowdfunding project, however it was also low for their overall film budget total of £500,000. There were varying levels of donation from £10 to £1000 and each tier would attract a different reward, from a DVD of the film to being invited to the film set, or receiving VIP tickets for the film premiere.

Kate continues: 'We gave ourselves 3 months to raise the figure and found that very little happened in this time. But we were able to extend. On reflection the reasons for this appeared to be a combination of our fundraising total being a drop in the ocean, compared to our film budget and that the lead time gave no element of urgency for raising the money.

'The pattern with crowdfunding appears to be that people either contribute at the beginning or end of the campaign. We learnt that doing as much prep before launching the campaign was crucial, so it benefited to keep the campaign short with a surge of people contributing up front and then others donating at the end to ensure you met your total (if your total wasn't reached then all donations would be returned to the investors). Thankfully we reached our total and money was received about a month later.' The film was shown on British television in 2015.

Crowdfunder

Crowdfunder, who work with Nesta, a government backed innovation charity supporting what they consider life-changing ideas, say they are the UK's largest crowdfunding network and have launched more than 3000 projects and raised more than £2m. They can, at best, they tell, raise £40k in just six days and they are particularly pleased to have helped the youngest crowdfunder Dylan Allman, 7, to raise money for his cookery book.

What is the legal status of crowdfunding in UK?

The Financial Conduct Authority set out rules for loan-based crowdfunding platforms in March 2014: 'The new rules for loan-based crowdfunding platforms will set "prudential requirements" for those businesses. They will have to put in place a certain amount of "financial resources" to underpin their business. The precise amount will depend on the total value of the loaned funds that are outstanding at the time that total is calculated.' They are being 'made subject to certain financial services rules and consumer protection requirements,' like other lenders/funders.

The Crowdfunding Accreditation for Platform Standards (CAPS)

CAPS is a programme set up by Crowdsourcing.org to protect both crowdfunders (people pledging or investing capital) and fundraisers (people raising capital). They are supported by an advisory council of leading platform operators and industry experts and their aim is to make sure high standards are kept by crowdfunding operations.

Who is the right crowdfunder for you?

Searching for which crowdfunder might be right for your project can feel like embarking on a walk through the confusing tunnels and pathways of a labyrinth. Clearly it makes sense to find one likely to attract people interested in what you are proposing, and for it to be a solidly based platform - which was the motivation of Alex Feldman, founder of CrowdsUnite (crowdsunite.com). He thought a way was needed to cut through the confusion, after the U.S. JOBS Act was passed, paving the way for legal equity crowd-funding from non-accredited investors.

So, his website is intended to offer guidance with reviews of crowdfunding sites. 'What I'm trying to become is a Yelp for the crowdfunding industry, a resource that anybody can use,' says Feldman, who won the accolade of being featured in *Entrepreneur* magazine. He believes there are more than 1,000 global crowd-funding sites in existence, of which they list almost 100, with a focus on U.S. sites that serve entrepreneurs.

Reviews

CrowdsUnite is a free website which offers a five-star scale of reviews, and users can filter searches by country, type of financing (debt, donation, equity or reward) and type of campaign (all or nothing vs. keep what you raise). The site lists the number of monthly visitors each platform receives and its fundraising fees.

Using a five-star scale, reviewers - who must include a link to their crowdfunding campaign - can rate a platform's customer service and ease of use and indicate whether they succeeded in raising money from strangers. Reviewers also offer written feedback about the platform.

In mid 2012 Alex Norton looked into crowdfunding for his procedural RPG (Role-Playing Game) *Malevolence: The Sword of Ahkranox*. But this first attempt did not go well. 'I made up a video for my product, slapped together a few screenshots and gameplay videos and left it there for a month on a crowdfunding site, expecting to find the account full of money at the end of it. The exercise was fruitless. Not only did it get to barely an eighth of what I needed financially, it copped a fair amount of negative publicity, which put me to thinking. My strategy for running my campaign was entirely wrong.'

So what did he need to do? He had a product, he says, 'but a rough one. It worked, but wasn't as pretty as it could be. And to make your project pretty is often the part that takes up most of your money, so that's what I looked to crowdfunding for. No matter how impressive something is technically, without the right shine it just becomes hard to "sell" to an audience.'

This next time he decided to try Kickstarter at the suggestion of one of the American members of his team but although he stresses what he tells about his own crowdfunding story is 'not an exact science', he did apply a scientific approach doing 'significant research on successful, crowd-funded projects,' and drew up a list of things he must do. He concludes broadly: 'It all comes down to how you sell your product, and how you sell yourself and your team as people.'

How you sell is all-important

Alex followed the guidance he now offers to us, 'Talk to those pledging and potential customers. Answer their questions when they have them and keep them engaged. Be aware of your target audience and gear every little thing you do towards them and only them. Be willing to put in the hours that it takes to make regular updates, answer all questions.

'Show the customer that the project is being made by people. Good quality, friendly, nice people. If they like you, they'll be more inclined to like what you're selling. Don't just show them why your product is special. Show them why it's special to YOU, and why it should be special to THEM.

'Write lots of updates. At LEAST 3 per week. Show you're working at it. Show how dedicated you are. Try and use video where possible. People respond to video. Get your best speaker onto it.'

This time the crowdfunding brought in 500% of his requested total. But as Alex found out: 'Not all campaigns work and it's not always your fault, or because your product is a bad one. Sometimes the planets just don't want to align for you, but a failure is only a failure if you don't learn from it. You can always try again.'

Little fraud in crowdfunding

I have not used crowdfunding and, although it's always a viable option if I have a project that needs backing, it is also important to realise that crowdfunding is not failsafe, a guaranteed pot of gold at the end of your efforts.

As Alex Norton told, his first attempt was a failure and some 60% of crowdfunding initiatives do not get the sum needed. One reviewer of this suggests 'these crowdfunders seem to seriously underestimate the amount of time they need to invest in getting their projects ready' and stresses the need for promotional groundwork before launching a campaign.

When this happens none of the donors pays out. But there is

integrity as Ethan Mollick from the University of Pennsylvania encouragingly notes. He found that fraud occurred very rarely. And potential crowdfunders might do well to look at the crowdfunding skills challenge website where they discuss in reasonable detail what you can usefully know about getting your crowdfunding initiative right. All this said, there are some wonderfully inspiring tales.

The Bicycle Academy, for example, is a wonderfully inventive project where they teach the skills for building a bike frame, then encourage you to build another for which they have a design that is suitable for use in Africa. They raised £40,000 in six days and they have been told that it's the fastest and most funded, reward-based crowdfunding campaign in the UK. They were selected on the basis of this as one of the top 20 startups in the UK for 2011.

Big thinking in funding

A bit of grandiose thinking here, but that is what is needed when it comes to securing money for Lifestyle Entrepreneurs these days. *Funding Circle* was created with the idea of revolutionising the outdated banking system and securing a better deal for everyone. They describe themselves as the world's leading marketplace exclusively focused on small businesses.

And they say, with understandable pride, that they have helped to generate more than £500 million of lending to small firms in the UK and the US, reaching the milestone just days after announcing a tie-up with Royal Bank of Scotland. They have also enabled businesses to borrow directly from people and organisations. More than £600m has been lent to 8,000 businesses in the UK and USA and they explain that businesses can borrow directly from a wide range of investors, including more than 40,000 people, the UK Government, local councils, a university and a number of financial organisations.

Start-up loans

Along with unemployment, particularly among the young, increasingly the Tory government is all too aware of how tricky the job market has been for young people wanting to launch into the world of work, so they set formed their Start Up loans scheme in 2012.

To get one you must be starting a new business, or have been trading for less than 12 months. Anyone over 18 and living in England, Northern Ireland, and Wales is eligible.

The average loan is around £6,000 although it can go to £10,000 with a fixed rate of interest currently set at 6%. You get just one Start Up Loan per person and must pay back the loan within 1-5 years.

Once you apply and your application is accepted, it will be assigned to a 'delivery partner' who will assess your business plan. If they then approve what you're doing, you get the loan and are assigned a mentor.

Suzanne Noble needed start-up money to launch her app Frugl for people wanting to enjoy London on a low budget. She tells with chatty enthusiasm of putting together the app she had always wanted with live music, comedy and club nights, walks and talks, sales and installations, all filtered by price and date. She was convinced there was enough of a gap in the market for this app to apply to Virgin start-ups, which is one of various sources for the loans.

Suzanne, who has spent several decades setting up and running successful small businesses, calculated it was worth doing for her project but muses:

'Like most things this government does, the money is just short of being helpful. Firstly, it hasn't really been devised to help tech businesses, as one of the criteria for being given the loan is the ability to generate revenue within 3 months of receiving the money. When you're developing a tech product, the revenue can take a while to come so you can see how this requirement could be problematic.

'The loan states that each 'founder' can receive a maximum of £10k, unsecured at 6% interest. This is not the best deal on the market but the scheme promotes itself by saying it can get you the money within 10 days of the application being received. In my case it took 6 long weeks and my loan manager having to go to the Director of Start-Up Loans (startuploans.co.uk) to get our loan approved. In any case, it has come with the perk of it being a Virgin loan, which gives me access to some top notch mentors. I have just been invited to a dinner for 20 comprised of the Virgin Board of Directors! So I am not going to complain.'

Loans for jobseekers

The government also offers loans to people over 18 and on a benefit scheme such as Job Seekers allowance to help them set up their own work. You may get a loan to help with start-up costs, a weekly allowance paid over 26 weeks plus help writing a business plan and mentoring. And they are keen to point out that it is not just the young getting the opportunities in this scheme. Over 9,000 businesses were started with this help by people aged over 50, and 7,000 by people with a disability (gov.uk/ government/ collections/ new-enterprise-allowance-campaign) and there are about 100 schemes under the grants section of the government website. To search for funding in the UK, the government website offers a search facility (gov.uk/business-finance-support-finder) and there are also private sources of funding here: betterbusiness-finance.co.uk.

Investors

Though a small business loan is a good starting point, seeking investors allows you more access to funds that you generally don't have to repay on a set schedule. However, it's not as though investors will give you funding without expecting anything in return, and you may need to relinquish some control of your business in order to work with certain investors. It also helps to prove that you have interest in your idea from family and friends (and others if possible). If family and friends aren't willing to financially back your idea, then why should an investor?

Angel investors

Angels can be found among an entrepreneur's family and friends, suggests *Investopedia*, the online investing magazine. They might provide a one-time injection of seed money or ongoing support when the company goes through difficult times. But others describe Angel Investors in tougher terms as affluent individuals who provide capital for a business start-up or in exchange for a convertible debt or ownership equity. They may be erstwhile entre-preneurs, and sometimes philanthropists, but they also may want a hand on the steering wheel of your enterprise.

Private lending

Financial writer Lil Sawyer knows the story: 'Well prepared entre-preneurs are walking into the banks with brilliant business ideas and well developed business plans - and are walking out empty-handed.' Yet she has seen how many of these same people find they can convince a private lender to give them the assistance they need.

These are people who have money and are on the look out for great business ideas, however, they will make the same stringent demand for a strong business plan as anyone else prepared to fund you. Nor are they more relaxed about the formalities, Sawyer points out:

'On the whole they will conduct a similar due diligence as the banks, and they will want contingency scenarios and realistic forecasts. But they do tend to be willing to invest in higher risk ventures because they are interested in the idea and more prepared to gamble than others.'

Business capital brokers may put you in touch with a private lender - they build up a dossier of people they consider promising and then try to match the applicant with someone appropriate.

Credit cards

Surveys of entrepreneurs frequently show that credit cards are among the most popular sources of startup financing, according to *Entrepreneur* magazine. But take pause before you choose to use your full line of credit to be up and running as soon as possible and hear Elaine Pofeldt at the creditcards.com online magazine. She knows the seductive blue skies talk:

'We've all read articles about entrepreneurs who borrowed their startup money on credit cards and built wildly profitable businesses. The most obvious advantage of credit card financing is that it's easily available if you already have good credit and cards in your name.

'However, for many entrepreneurs, using credit cards as a main form of financing is very risky. If the business fails, they will be saddled with debt for which they are personally responsible - regardless of whether they have taken out business or personal credit cards. This is because both types of cards typically require a personal guarantee.'

For the *Wild Card Brewery*, cutting loose from steady earnings was 'an act of faith and folly we often thought,' Andrew says, remembering the nerve wracking business of using his credit card to raise capital to get the beer business going on a wing and a prayer.

They were all working in full-time jobs during the two years they developed a recipe for pale ale akin to their favourite beer from Nottingham. They studied brewing from textbooks and created the first 200 pints in William and Jaega's kitchen. They put it into different bottles with different logos. Then came the biggest challenge: they got orders that needed delivering within a couple of months. At which point, Andrew explains, he took his credit card as the only one of the three with a good credit rating, bought the ingredients, hired equipment for a day, and together they worked demonically to fulfil the orders.

They banked on getting paid promptly by their customer so that they could pay off at least some of the loan immediately and at the same time put some of their earning aside to make beer for their next orders. It was not that easy. Payments came late, creditors were recalcitrant and they were blessedly glad Andrew still had a job.

You need to be certain you will get paid according to legal strictures and the understanding by clients of how you work, is how it should be done if you must use credit cards, in the view of Nat Wasserstein, chief restructuring officer at *Lindenwood Associates*, a crisis management firm based in New York City. Not least because credit cards are an expensive way of borrowing and you could run into repayment difficulties almost before you have started (creditcards.com/credit-card-news/fund-startup-business-risks-1585.php).

I realise what a daunting task fundraising appears to be. So you need hold on tight to the knowledge that good ideas, from the frankly off-the-wall, the quirky, and the inspirational, to hard-nosed product based enterprises, and plenty of philanthropic projects, do get money to start up if not more, from the ways suggested here. It may also be the case that you can reduce your overheads considerably, as I have done, meaning investment can be something that comes later, or is not even necessary because you can fund your own project independently like Jack Cator, founder of the VPN service Hide My Ass, did.

7

TECH SAVVINESS

A toolbox of technological know-how is as important as anything you can have. However much some might yearn for handwritten letters, the fact is most people you deal with will want and expect communications that can be opened on a screen, are quick and easy to read, and that can be altered by them. You will also probably benefit from the considerable time saved by being able to correct a document as you go on, rather than relying on Tippex when your effort emerges from the typewriter imperfections writ large.

And yes, this applies even if you are a landscape gardener, have a craft stall at a market, or offer a home cleaning service. Businesses of every kind that succeed these days almost invariably have a website, an email address, and will send out information produced on a computer. Online activity is the engine to so many operations these days, particularly with with more and more people shopping for goods and services online.

Tech savviness
Understanding how to use a computer and going beyond the most basic word processing skills is a number one skill these days. You may not consider yourself a dinosaur if you use an old fashioned typewriter to produce letters, invoices, mail outs, but chances are the world around you will think just that.

You need to understand how vital the Internet is and put the time and effort in to not only be online, but keep up to date with how to best use it for your earning stream(s). Below is a list of things I believe are essential in your 'tecchie toolbox' as a modern day LE.

Learn how to effectively research online

Learning how to research online properly, especially things relevant to your area of business, is an absolute must. It will let you assess your competition's marketing techniques, popularity, and what not to do as well as what you should be doing as a minimum to stay in business. It will also let you reinvent yourself as an entrepreneur if an income stream suddenly disappears as you'll see when things look like they are going South before they actually do.

Keep up to date with trends

Following trends through things like keeping an eye on Search Engine Optimisation (SEO), forums for SEO tips, following experts in your field, and knowing how and where to look for content, products or services for your own business purposes, will all help you thrive as a LE.

Keep your ducks in a straight line

As you can imagine, researching in any form (and running a business!) can get messy quickly. I use Mind Maps, bookmarks and online tools like Evernote (evernote.com), Wunderlist (wunderlist.com) and even YouTube playlists (lists of videos essentially) to structure and organise any content, services and websites I come across that will be of use later. This goes for not only physical things, but also organising your computer folders as well. Have a think about how you will logically extend your folder structure as you accumulate more information i.e. start general with folders like 'Design', 'Finance' and 'Deliverables' then go more specific with subfolders. With a folder like 'Finance', you might have subfolders like 'Tax', 'Invoices' and 'Receipts' etc. Believe me, it will make your life infinitely easier if you can quickly and easily find the things you need by dipping in and out of well-organised folders.

Master your software

If you're not familiar with essential software like Word, Excel and Powerpoint (or similar products like Open Office or Apple's suite of iLife tools), then you should teach yourself with online resources or taking classes whether online or offline at places like Udemy (udemy.com) and Microsoft's own resources (support.office.com - look for *Office training, videos, and tutorials*). I make sure I'm up to speed with any software that is important for what I want to do, like Photoshop for editing images that I use to market myself online and iMovie for quickly putting together promotional videos for YouTube or even save my voice over clients' videos with my voice over in place. There are so many free resources to learn almost anything online, that there really is no excuse these days to not learn how to use important software other than putting in a bit of effort. For coding, things like w3schools.com, codecademy.com and searching for solutions to coding problems on Stackoverflow (stackoverflow.com) and its sister sites are great.

Gone in a Flash

One of the things you may not have thought about, yet is incredibly important, is the topic of backing up important data and files before emergencies happen. If you're developing income streams that are primarily online or building up a database of customers on your computer, this becomes even more important. How you store that data can also have legal ramifications if you're cataloguing sensitive data like personal details and credit card numbers etc..

My 'process' involves using the free version of dropbox.com to synchronise a folder on my computer that contains all the work I'm currently working on. I use the Dropbox app on my iPhone to pass files to clients via Dropbox all the time, but you need an Internet connection to back things up. I archive all my audio, video and graphics work on an external hard drive that I call 'the master'. Because 'the master' is so important, I clone it every 2-3 days to two other 4tb external hard drives. Having a location that is separate to your workplace to store the occasional backup is wise in case there's a fire or some other catastrophe.

Break down tasks into bite-size chunks

If you are intent on using things like social media to promote yourself, be realistic about how much you can take on. Start small (i.e. you might want to start just with a Facebook and YouTube account) and then scale up if necessary. Try breaking down your tasks, such as preparing videos to post on YouTube, writing regular tweets etc. into small bits so that you might spend 30 mins to 1 hour on them each day. Even better, prepare them in a way that they can easily be outsourced in the future.

Strength in community

One of the toughest things LEs tend to say, if they are working solo, is that they feel isolated, out of touch with what the world around is talking about, and that all this affects confidence. I know about all of these, and I also know how immensely valuable it has been to tap into online communities, as well as offline gatherings of friends and work colleagues to shoot the breeze and compare notes. But along with the pleasure of making human contacts you can communicate with easily and quickly, the online communities are also a resource for letting people know what you are doing, selling yourself, and attracting clients.

When I first dipped my toes in multi-stream earning, I was taken back by the high level of activity I found on forums, social media channels, blogs and other communities including networking events near me. There are vibrant communities in every niche, not just music, and many people within them want to help each other succeed, whether that's by contributing to the topic of a blog post, suggesting improvements to a product or helping the author with general supportive feedback.

If you work from home like I do, not only are these kinds of communities enjoyable socially and break you out of feeling alone, they can be a source of inspiration and new clients or a place to develop business partnerships, friendships, share tips that have worked (or not worked) and vent your frustrations.

For example, Miriam Lahage runs a business helping start-ups and a more general consultancy. She says, 'It's nice to have people who are on their own journey around you. It can be a very solitary move, especially at the very beginning, so finding people allows you to commiserate and have a number one and number two when it's time for you to build a team like finding a co-founder. And with the network that you've created...it is usually where you find the right people to work with.'

Miriam spends a third of her time with the businesses she's working with, a third of the time meeting new people and the last third learning new things. When she was talking to her friends at Google and Facebook, she went in and introduced herself, got to know what they were doing and got access to the right people that way. This kind of networking, she says, creates a situation where one helps the other and the other helps you.

Active member of the community

Pamela Ferguson, a 70 year-old multi-stream earner who works in complementary health and as a writer, agrees that it can be a solitary thing working for yourself. 'Being self-employed, I have found it vital to be an active member of the community, to interact a lot with neighbours and with local shop owners, folks in the bank and post office. This has been my pattern in London, New York, San Francisco, and even near Zurich, and especially now in Austin! I would find isolation killing...but perhaps that's just my personality!'

There's an interesting theory about how even a small strong and dedicated community can support your lifestyle by senior Maverick at *Wired* magazine, Kevin Kelly. He believes that with 1000 fans, a content creator can make enough to live off:

'A creator, such as an artist, musician, photographer, craftsperson, performer, animator, designer, videomaker, or author – in other words, anyone producing works of art – needs to acquire only 1,000 True Fans to make a living...A True Fan is defined as someone who will purchase anything and everything you produce. They will drive

200 miles to see you sing. They will buy the super deluxe re-issued hi-res box set of your stuff even though they have the low-res version…they can't wait till you issue your next work. They are true fans.' (Kevin Kelly, kk.org, kk.org/ thetechnium/ 1000-true-fans/)

Connect directly

He goes further to say that you need to connect with your 'True Fans' directly and that you should assume conservatively that 'your True Fans will each spend one day's wages per year in support of what you do,' even though in reality they may spend more.

Long-lasting relationships are really what generate regular income in any business and is something that Lorenzo Sapora, who is a printer, developer and designer on People per Hour, quickly found out after joining. He says that producing quality work along with personalised messages and friendly conversations has translated into long term clients.

And communities can also be useful as a passive income stream and building 'brand awareness' through user comments and people sharing your content. Matt Harris, like many other YouTube content creators, earns not only from the advertising that appears on his videos, but through affiliate links to his music that he sells and puts underneath the visuals of all his videos, general download sales from places like iTunes and occasionally direct licensing when a client gets in touch with special circumstances.

In fact, from the 25,000 or so YouTube subscribers that Matt has built up so far (youtube.com/user/alumoaudio), he has reached a situation where the potential to earn comes from four different sources:

- The sale of his music if they buy the track he links to.
- Advertising that appears on his own channel.
- Referring viewers to a site where they can buy his music (even if they buy someone else's media, he earns a referral amount as an affiliate).
- From people stealing his music and posting it on their own

videos via a system that scans YouTube videos and puts ads on them if the uploader hasn't purchased a license to use his music. The enthusiastic comments left on his videos from his fans also helps feed into his sales.

Marketing as connection

If you're used to the 9-5 approach to work, and don't work in sales or marketing of course, then promoting yourself may seem a daunting and uncomfortable task. However, it's an essential component of multi-stream earning as people need to know what you're offering if they're to buy from you or invest time or money in your work.

You should think of marketing as a way of connecting with people who share an interest in your product or service rather than as a chore. The old model of 'the hard sell' still works in some sectors, but it is very quickly becoming outdated and replaced by new tactics that engage audiences rather than bluntly direct sales pitches at them, particularly with the 'entertain-me-fast' millennial generation taking charge as the next generation of consumers.

And that can be a fun process. Think of marketing as a conversation with your audience, not necessarily a 'friendship' (although I've made good friendships by reaching out in this way), but as a way of sharing mutual interests with your community, and you'll likely form strong long-lasting relationships with your followers.

Although a lot of the techniques here are online, remember that a lot of the concepts can be applied offline.

When communities go bad

While the Internet can provide a wonderful place to exchange ideas, form new relationships and build trust with your followers, there is also a dark side to it that you should be aware of. Places like YouTube and Twitter are notorious for 'trolls' (individuals who leave inflammatory, provocative and often offensive responses), and they can be particularly damaging to the cohesion of your community if you're not careful.

If you do something that is controversial and it is shared on social media, you can expect to see some reactions both good and bad. For example, take celebrity chef Paula Deen, who was fired by the Food Network after she allegedly made some racist comments and they went viral on social media. With over 1 million followers on Twitter, a website, blog and YouTube channel, Paula unsurprisingly received a lot of remarks from her followers.

And the more popular you become, the more likely nasty comments will appear on your channel. However, Swedish-born Felix Arvid Ulf Kjellberg, aka PewDiePie on YouTube, has turned this kind of community input on its head. He took a bunch of derogatory comments and put them in a video for his channel and his since been benefiting from advertising revenue in the process (look for 'Reading Mean Comments' on PewDiePie's channel on YouTube or go type in this URL int your browser: https://goo.gl/pLUIzR).

With over 12 million views on that video alone, it's an inspired way of connecting more with his true followers, getting new subscribers through people sharing the video and, at the same time, deflecting the negativity from the 'trolls.'

So how do I get started?

If you want to connect with an audience, you need to think about where they are. Here are some questions you should be asking yourself:

- Where do my customers hang out? Are they primarily online or offline?
- Are there any events that are related to what I do that my target audience will be at?
- Do they participate in forums (whether physical or online)?
- Are there any industry networking events happening soon?
- What promotional materials do I already have like business cards or leaflets?

As a budding composer, there are various events in my diary to attend such as the Cannes film festival, Develop (a video game development conference), Screened Music Masterclasses, and other industry networking events where I'll meet people working in films and games whether directors, producers, music library owners or even just other composers.

You'll find you have opportunities to get known with regular attendees and connect with other successful entrepreneurs that are often willing to lend a hand to people starting out. I recommend you reach out in this way as I've often had to break out of my comfort zone, doing things like cold-calling and presenting my work in front of strangers for feedback, to improve the quality of my work as well as my marketing skills. But it's almost always created more opportunities or put me in contact with people that can help me with my cause.

Even if things are slow to start, try to stay positive and experiment with things, it's the only way to find out what works for you, as Natalia Talkowska says:

'I thought everything would be great when I started working on my own, but when things didn't happen I felt very low. That made me open up to other people looking for suggestions, making changes to what I was actually offering and listening to people. I would say it's hard work, but be open to suggestions and new ideas, don't stay in a bubble, try things out. Some things will work, some won't. If you see the ideas that are working polish them up and test the market.'

If you prepare your psychological mindset and have a plan for how you want to approach marketing, and indeed your business as a whole, then your life will become much easier as you can see clearly where you're going with it all.

Again, I find Mind Maps very useful in this respect: I sketch out what I want to try, number the branches of the most promising ideas to test and work through them. My Mind Maps also evolve the more I learn about my audience and their needs.

Competition

Being tech savvy is an important part of keeping competitive because so many things, like routine emails, filing digital documents such as receipts and invoices, and even sending your work documents / files, are online these days. And in order to stay afloat in any market, you need to think competitively. Indeed, it needs to be a repeating theme in your head even if you don't aspire to be the kind of flailing fisted competitive dealer keen to crush those in the way underfoot.

I've had to identify who my competition is and raise my game even in the royalty-free music arena which has traditionally been considered 'cheap', easy to compete in, and have a low threshold to entry i.e. you needed to merely create some fairly 'low quality' music and you were in.

Bear in mind, too, that in some cases, and particularly online, you may be up against people who have far lower living costs than you, meaning competition based on price is fierce. Describing an ad on 99designs, Donna Freedman from GetRichSlowly.org says:

'Depending on your specialty it might be tough to earn consistently liveable wages…witness an ad that begins: "I will write five high-quality articles of 500 and more words within short time for $19." That pitch continued in poorly phrased English, with punctuation that made me twitchy. Yet it's pretty common, since $19 USD probably goes further in whatever country is home to that "high quality" writer.'

Competing on price is a dangerous game as there will always be people willing to go lower than you meaning it can turn into an endless downwards-spiralling bidding war. Far more sustainable is the approach of improving the quality of what you're offering so you can charge reasonable amounts that fit your living costs while also staying competitive.

Gerard Jones, an award-winning entrepreneur football coach, leader in coach education, and founder of the Gerard School of Football, had a passion for football as a 19-year-old, encouraged and coached by his father. He had wanted to be a player but soon recognised he would not make the grade. Instead of letting himself be too disappointed he decided to see the situation as a step taking him in the direction of what he should be doing. That, he decided, was coaching.

So the training he had gained as a player was valuable, but he turned then to skilling himself up as a coach in order to get a competitive foothold in this career. He started one-to-one training of the children of parents keen for them to progress and, in the first year, work was busy enough that he took on two helpers and earned something of a reputation for being good.

He set up his venture in 2009 knowing that he had to be 'the best of the best' in this highly competitive line of work, and he succeeded in becoming one of the top 100 Best Business Start-Ups in the UK in 2010. That dedicated skilling up led to him partnering Arsenal Football Club in running the Arsenal Soccer School's programme in Yorkshire.

Gerard gives a loud scoffing laugh at the idea that he might have achieved this without always keeping his eye on being competitive, offering more than the chap behind him.

'You have to know you are the best and do everything you can to demonstrate that. It's why people want you and what they pay for.'

Christine Fogg, who trained as a nurse, left in frustration at the way the NHS worked. She recognised that if she was going to work for herself she needed to equip herself with skills that would be really competitive in the marketplace. She chose to do a business diploma and supported herself through this with cleaning jobs and some nursing of HIV patients.

From this work she was asked to run a small HIV organisation and was fairly quickly made CEO. As her children grew up she wanted to broaden her work, so she did a coaching course where she met three women with whom she set up a network, which generated some coaching work. She explains how that led to coaching work for the charity wing of the Cass Business School.

'Even so, I realised that to be competitive and keep ahead I needed to develop my skills further, that I would not be skilled up enough to be really competitive without this. So I did a masters which gave me more credibility, particularly with Cass.

'Once I felt more confident I started approaching people and having conversations about what I could offer them with my social work coaching experience and new skills. I was asked to help with a new start-up because my masters had given me the knowledge to understand how the project should work, the government implications, marketing and how to work strategically. So it was very clear how upping my skills had given me a competitive edge.'

Promotion - vital not vanity

It is startling how many of us have been told from a young age that we shouldn't show off; we shouldn't push ourselves forward to be noticed; that discretion and modesty are great values.

Up to a point that is wide guidance. Kids who are forever telling the world they are the best at everything, cleverer and smarter than anyone else, are all too likely to end up pretty isolated because the self-interested boaster is not usually the greatest company.

But it is a very different story if, as an adult - young or mature - you are setting up your own business, offering services and skills. Then it is important to tell the world just how good you are; why you offer something better than the opposition; why they should choose you over the competition.

Which is where marketing and self-promotion come in as the tools you will need to let the world know you are out there, with something to offer you are proud of and sincerely hope they will want. So your start-up is a time to push modesty and self-effacement out the way and get blowing your own trumpet.

You should think of self-promotion as an *investment* in your multi-stream business, but it doesn't mean it should be your only focus. And although engaging in self-promotion can be time-consuming, it doesn't have to be *your* time - you can get other people to put together your marketing materials through services like Fiverr and People per Hour so you have more time to do things like improve your product or service, or maybe just take some time off!

But more important than working harder is working *smarter*. Think carefully about how you can maximise your efforts so things like creating a YouTube video doesn't just get a few views, but totally engages your audience because you've carefully thought about who they are, their needs and their interests.

As we saw with his 25k+ subscribers, Matt Harris has done this particularly well with his YouTube channel (youtube.com/ user/ alumoaudio) because he thought carefully about his demographic, put his advertising cap on, and gradually built up a strong and engaged audience who buy into his vision and market for him as they are so enthused by what he's offering. As a result, he gets a steady stream of music sales.

Self-promotion

Self-promotion should be about small regular marketing efforts rather than one big push to get people's attention. The 'drip-feed' approach of giving your audience focused relevant content (often useful, informative or entertaining) is what will get you noticed as you can build up a conversation with them over time and build trust. While you certainly can become an overnight success if one of your tweets, YouTube videos or Facebook posts goes viral, it's not a sustainable way of building up a loyal following.

The frequency with which you release content is important too and you can only find out what works for your audience by testing it - do you see a drop off in interest at certain times of day? If you're using Twitter, are four tweets a day too much? Are people watching all of your videos or disappearing after a few seconds? A lot of YouTube vloggers who make their living off advertising revenue, sponsorships and product placements etc. in their shows release videos to their subscribers two to three times a week. Some even release videos every day, like reality vlogger Judy Travis whose channel It's Judy's Life is a daily update on her and her family's life (itsjudytime.com).

Choosing the right platform to self-promote on is also important. Not only are certain services geared more towards particular demographics, but the audiences there are expecting content to be presented a certain way, meaning your marketing should adapt accordingly. Pinterest, for example, is a photo-sharing site with a large female following whose users share things like the latest trends in fashion, delicious images of cupcakes, arts and crafts, unusual recipes and even photo-based make-up tutorials.

YouTube, on the other hand, has everything from tutorials, pranks and DIY videos plus a lot of people with very short attention spans, so you would shape your content differently (like planning a beginning, middle and end for your videos) to get the best results and keep people engaged. If you're interested in learning about YouTube techniques, subscribe to Tim Schmoyer's channel (youtube.com/user/VideoCreatorsTV) who is an expert in everything YouTube. Lastly, LinkedIn has a more professional crowd and can be a fantastic way to build links between industry professionals. No cat videos to be found there.

Michael Bihovsky adopts a lightly self-mocking tone when describing his use of social media, but in truth his Facebook presence is very well orchestrated. 'I am cognizant that I am not nearly as active on social media as I "should" be - I pretty much only stick to Facebook (where I happily accept the friend requests of fans that I have never met, who often end up being the most vocal commenters and sharers when I do post content). I have been told that I should be spending much more time on Twitter and create a LinkedIn account, but frankly so much of my energy is already going to my computer that I can't stomach the idea of having to spend any more.

'That said, when I am trying to gain momentum for a particular project, I do use Facebook regularly, and especially try to encourage others to share the content as well. The success of my 'One Grain More' video, at least in its early stages, was almost entirely due to my friends sharing the video, and then their friends, and their friends, etc. It got bigger and bigger, which is how it became 'viral.'

'As for how 'brazen' I choose to be - well, I am firmly of the mindset that nobody can market you better than yourself (at least when you're on a budget), but at the same time, I try not to be annoying in repeatedly posting the same content. So if I do repeat content, I always try to do so with a new twist – for example, a new article that came out about the project, or a behind-the-scenes joke.

That sort of thing. I also am very dependent upon my mailing list and website.'

Andrew, William and Jaega of the *Wild Card Brewery* have absorbed the message that social media is, these days, a vital part of becoming a known brand. William tells:

'We use Facebook, Twitter and YouTube for our promotions. We knew that being a start-up this was important and it took quite a lot of our time and energy.'

Streamlining your efforts

Like any well-oiled machine, carrying out repetitive tasks become manageable if you set things up correctly. By doing things like reinvesting some of what you earn from an income stream, as I do with the passive income I get from my sales on royalty-free music websites, you can create an autonomous 'cyclical' marketing system that feeds back into your business.

What that means is you should be looking to *automate* parts of your business, like marketing and fulfilling orders, as much as possible. You want to be concentrating on the things you enjoy while still keeping in touch with your audience and you can do that by setting up systems that require as little effort or input from yourself as possible.

Depending on what you're offering, that can mean things like:

- Setting up auto-responder emails on your website that deliver useful content throughout the year to your subscribers.
- Collecting contact details and sending a personalised letter or email after a purchase that cross-sells something else you offer, gives them a freebie or maybe a discount.
- Up-selling products (prompting someone to buy more) automatically when someone is checking out.
- Hiring in people to market for you through services like People per Hour, Fiverr or Upwork or a local person you trust.
- Sharing a live video-stream of an event you host on YouTube

(you just press record and the rest is streamed and saved on YouTube).
- Creating a process where user-generated content (UGC) becomes part of your marketing strategy.

That last point can be particularly powerful. Giants like Google do this with their services like YouTube and Google+ and Instagram, Pinterest, Twitter and Facebook - all use UGC to feed into their services, build interest and brand loyalty. Without this content, those services would actually be worthless in many ways. Look at how many videos Google releases on YouTube or the number of posts shared on Facebook that are by Facebook - how popular are they? Not very, the celebrities on these channels are the users as they are creating the content.

But you don't need to be a giant company to do the same. In fact, you can use these free services as a platform to let users share their experience of your product or service by asking them to tweet content to your Twitter profile, post their favourite photos on Facebook or Instagram, leave reviews on your website, or even get people to respond to a YouTube video.

Getting others to market you for a cut

Something that is huge in the passive income model is affiliate selling. In a nutshell, affiliate systems let other people generate leads or market your product or service for you in exchange for a cut of the earnings. Web hosting companies like Bluehost and Hostgator are popular as affiliates can earn decent money referring people to their hosting packages via URLs that track who sent the customer. It's a bit like a company asking, 'how did you find out about us?', the unique URL you're given tells the company that you sent the customer there and therefore get a cut of the sale.

Places like Clickbank have become popular because they allow people to sell other people's products, particularly informational products like eBooks and courses, and so may be something you want to consider if you intend to earn a passive income. Letting others sell your products can also help you build an email list and generate new leads from new customers.

Paying to extend your reach

Paying for advertising works, otherwise why would so much money be spent decade after decade on sending out messages and images designed to fill our minds with the idea that we want them? And in the same way in today's digitised world, it is why people continue to invest in things like Google Ads, Facebook ads, Twitter ads, StumbleUpon ads, and putting web banner advertising slots on popular news sites like CNN, Forbes and Huffington Post. And advertisers now appear on almost every device we use these days such as smart phones, iPads, and computers, to get a mention of who they are and what they do under our eyes.

So people just like you now have the potential to reach a global market relatively easily and cheaply, but that doesn't mean you can put together any old campaign and expect returns. Just like with any kind of marketing, you need to have a set budget, know what you're doing, or hire in talent if you don't know how to leverage and monitor results.

Film producer Kate Cook says that dedicating money to marketing has been important for her film *Leave to Remain*:

'We put aside some of the film budget to employ a dedicated Online Producer who would manage all of our social media and oversee making the offline/online contacts in order to drive them to the Buzzbnk page. By doing this in tandem with our actual filming gave it real momentum and we found that as our deadline neared there was a clear surge of support.'

If you've had a moment to browse through some of the sites for outsourcing that we've mentioned, you may have seen that you can buy traffic for your site as well as Twitter followers, Facebook likes and YouTube subscribers.

Be wary of these types of services as they can get you blacklisted by Google for gaming the system if you abuse them. However, you might want to consider a little helping hand just to get you started or drive traffic to a landing page on your website to do things like build an email list (just remember to 'hide' this page from search engines by using your robots.txt file so it's not considered when ranking your page - see robotstxt.org/ robotstxt.html for how to do that).

Networking

Reaching out offline is as important in promotion, if not more, than online. The global access people now have to communicate online means that the competition to be heard is higher than ever, so meeting in person gives you an added edge.

Getting out and connecting with people if you work from home also reduces the risk of cutting yourself off from the real world too much. Natalia Talkowska says:

'Confidence builds up with time. When you see people like what you do and they need your services, that gives you confidence. The earlier you can grow your confidence the better because when you walk into that room and people see that you have no confidence you are on the losing side. What else is important is your body language, how you speak to people, how you look and present yourself. Even if you don't have confidence pretend that you do.'

Organising meetings and networking may feel a little uncomfortable in the beginning if you're not used to it, but it's very worthwhile. Some of my most solid contacts have come from meeting people in person as you bypass a lot of the 'distrust' that people have when meeting you online. They know who they're dealing with. And so do you.

8

GETTING GOING

It's good, isn't it, to be seen as someone winning a bit of prestige for breaking with the conventional wisdom that getting yourself a job, developing a stiff upper lip, and building businesses that others run, is the thing you should aspire to. And even better when it is someone at the cutting edge of youthful entrepreneurship, in this case Neeta Patel at the New Entrepreneurs Foundation, who says:

'I think there's a peer thing going on, the kudos of being an entrepreneur in your group. It's great…In the old days we used to look up to the people that got into Goldman Sachs' management scheme, because they had so much money…Now I think generation Y really admire entrepreneurs. Because they've seen so many of them, they've seen tech entrepreneurs (on programmes like Dragons' Den) - it adds to the acceptability of entrepreneurialism.'

Work smarter not harder

Multi-stream earning really can allow you to shape life to your own working rhythm. It can give you space for those family commitments, pleasure-seeking activities and free up time to relax. However, while it is a thoroughly positive approach to work life, rigorous and life-enhancing, it is not a way of side-stepping effort as the hippy approach tended to be seen. In fact, those espousing the LE way know they may well have to work very hard indeed. But it allows you to work smarter, not harder, because of the flexibility and control you ultimately have over your work life.

This said, the way we operate as a LE needs a clearly designed structure, a work plan that suits you, and you need to be absolutely realistic about the practicalities you'll need to observe. My life as a multi-stream earner has been made a lot easier by planning for and adapting to the practical realities of this way of earning. Organising myself has saved me a lot of stress and time, and I recommend you do it too to minimise disruptions to your workflow.

Where will you work

The number of people working from home has grown by more than 21 per cent in the past decade, according to the Live Work Network, and seven out of ten of these run their own businesses. Shrinking opportunities in the workplace, unemployment, state-of-the-art technology taking over office jobs, and a wish to cut out commuting and improve work-life balance and quality of life, are among the reasons that close on a quarter of the workforce, and counting, is making a radical shift in the way the workplace looks.

As a Lifestyle Entrepreneur you will, like me, probably want to use your home as your workplace. The advantages are clear: you do not have to pay for an office; you do not have to commute; you can make lunch in your own kitchen; you have more free time for fun and family if chunks of each day are not spent being transported to and from work. But there may be drawbacks too: if you don't have a room to turn into a dedicated office you may have to work in the bedroom, the living room, the kitchen or some other dual-purpose place and this is not ideal. But if it is the only possibility, then try to organise a desk and storage space that is separated from the room's other activities and make it very clear that they are not to be touched by anyone except you.

Lucy McCarraher lives in rural East Anglia in the home where she has brought up children 'for a very long time'. Her eldest is 31, the youngest 10, and she cannot imagine giving up the physical and psychological freedom her lifestyle gives for a formal job, no matter how well remunerated. And the advantage to being a tried and tested LE is, clearly, that she knows how she works, that she meets commitments and so she tells: 'I make my own rules, set my own schedules, be my own person, wear my own clothes, do my own thing.' She may well take a couple of hours off to do family food shopping or go for a walk, but she will make sure she puts in the hours required to meet commissions in time.

Finding sources of work

Finding people and companies to work with or who will buy your service or product is obviously an essential part of multi-stream earning. Without them, you would have no market to sell to and therefore no income!

If you're looking to earn offline, then it's worth starting by looking for local businesses or individuals who will be interested in what you're offering in places like the Yellow Pages, local business directories, and local newspapers. Contact old companies you've worked with as well as new companies as, assuming you've had good dealings with them previously, you can build a trusting relationship far quicker than cold-calling new ones.

As well as looking for potential clients in places like business directories, it's worth listing yourself in them as well to bring new business in. A technique that has worked for me is reaching out to companies who have a clear need, such as a website, or where I can improve what they already have in place significantly, as it's easier to convince people to act on something they need resolved.

It helps if what you're offering is likely to bring in a return on investment as most people are only looking to spend if they'll gain something in return. For example, you could go to a local window cleaning firm, plumber or junk removal company that didn't have a website and offer them your services (building the site, providing content, design etc.).

A method I came across via a friend was to quickly clone a previous site I'd built, replace a few parts specific to the client I was targeting, and explain how I could give them that type of website for a set fee. I've done this a couple of times successfully and it's effective as clients like to see a finished product, can see that you have incentive and that getting online can be affordable.

If you have a hobby you enjoy, think hard about how it might be turned into a way of earning; pick your friends' brains and turn to anyone you know with good business nous for ideas. Chances are if you are very enthusiastic about the thing you are trying you will give it the best possible shot with your efforts and enjoy the process.

Earning online

Internet trading is very big business these days. Online selling, whether it is long established stores setting up online sales or start-ups, understand that online offers the possibility of reaching customers who might never go near a shop or local service you are offering.

If you're looking to earn online, then there are a bunch of websites that are worth looking into. I've found the following useful in freelancing services to people globally but also finding other providers who have helped me complete jobs for previous clients:

Fiverr (www.fiverr.com)
People per Hour (www.peopleperhour.com)
Upwork (previously oDesk: www.odesk.com)
Freelancer (www.freelancer.com)
3to30 (www.3to30.com)
Guru (www.guru.com)
Elance (www.elance.com)
TaskRabbit (www.taskrabbit.com)
99designs (www.99designs.com)

I've also got future business leads from these sites as people have put me in touch with other companies through word-of-mouth following a business transaction, so these sites can be a good source for generating your own leads. If you're musically inclined, then you might be interested in three royalty-free music sites I regularly earn money from (currently around $500-600 a month):

AudioJungle (audiojungle.net)
Pond5 (pond5.com)
LuckStock (luckstock.com)

There are hundreds if not thousands of other places to earn online, and the lists above are far from exhaustive, but be careful to do some research into whether they are credible or not.

What to charge

This can be tricky. If you are working for yourself you have to weigh up what you are worth, whether you feel confident charging that amount, overhead costs like materials, and if you can undercut the competition while still making what you need and so on. It may be worth spending a bit of time thinking through these things, seeing how the competition are pitching their fees, and if you have experience from a previous job charging for the same type of work.

Some important things to consider are:

- How much do you need to earn to cover your operating costs and survive? Remember to consider *all* your monthly overheads.
- What do you consider a reasonable amount considering the type of work?
- Are you going to charge per project, or per hour?
- What are your competitors charging?
- Can you come up with an average hourly earnings rate based on previous jobs?
- Can you factor in a profit margin? Would 20%, 40% or even 100% work?

If you want something a bit more in-depth and based on existing research, then you could look at the books like *The Writer's Market* and *The Photographer's Market*, which report on what markets in a particular niche pay.

Check rates

The website Coroflot (coroflot.com/designsalaryguide) is also a useful indicator of rates for designers and visual creatives, but if you're really stuck, you might like to try Motivapp (motivapp.com/freelance-hourly-rate-calculator), which is a free website to calculate your rate.

While your rate might be higher than you expect if you've been in a full-time job previously, remember that your overheads do need to be covered. As I stressed earlier, you should make sure you *earn more than you spend*.

In some cases, your base rate might be decided for you by the entity you trade through. On *Fiverr* for example, you deal in multiples of $5 and are limited to certain amounts depending on how well you've been doing on the site. The incentive they've built into their model to keep you trading is to 'unlock' levels so you can charge more money the more you earn.

Top Seller

I'm currently a Top Seller on Fiverr which allows me to create 'add-ons' for extras to my voice-over gigs that let people pay, e.g. $10 or $20 extra for things like longer word counts, 24-hour delivery and adding background music. Like many sellers, my plan is to increase my rate by offering fewer words for more money as my popularity increases.

While that may seem counter-intuitive, top sellers continue to sell despite offering 'less' because they have customers enthusing about the quality of their work and have a strong record to back it up (like many sales and a high feedback rating). People pay for quality and are persuaded by someone's 'approval rating' online as it's an indicator of trust, so getting those two factors right can lead to a continuous stream of work.

And before you think that $5 is very little to charge, bear in mind that these micro-payments can add up due to multiple sales from high demand and repeat customers. Take the New York-based actor and voice-over artist Linnea Sage (fiverr.com/ linneas88), who earns two-thirds of her income from previous customers and pockets around $2,000 a month through *Fiverr*. You might think of it as the same principle behind phone app and eBook sales, whose authors cash in from multiple $1.99 sales. 10 sales might not be much, but at 1000, you've made $1999. If you think that's a lot, think about the traffic some of these sites get, like Amazon, whose traffic SimilarWeb (similarweb.com) estimates can reach 972 million visits a month.

At first it might be uncomfortable charging higher rates than you're used to. I remember being very nervous about raising my freelance rates for web development considering other cheaper alternatives exist. Then I started to write down what I was offering for my rate and it became clear I was oversupplying considerably for the fee I was charging. Something that also helped me decide on a freelance rate was committing to earning no less than my age in pounds sterling (per hour) as it separated me from the emotion of how clients might react.

Create structure

A very detailed schedule may sound mundane as the approach of a brave new work pioneer, but it is one of the most effective ways that I know of giving yourself a clear view of what you want to achieve and how you hope to do this. I described the Mind Map as a valuable tool for working out how I can create a multi-stream work hub and it can also be a useful organisational tool for day-to-day activities. You can write the main activity and then put all the affiliated activities in lines coming off it. This works well if you have work, as with my music, where there are two or three different projects coming from the one source. By drawing up a Mind Map I see very clearly what I need to do and then I put an approximate time on each strand for how long I think it should take.

This schedule should list projects you plan to work on alongside all the tasks that are involved in this work, even the smallest such as making sure your technology is working to speed, or having a notebook and pen to hand. It is surprising how often jotting down a thought, taking down a bit of information or telephone number by hand, and so on, are part of what we do.

It's also good to define when 'work' actually is, as you'll improve your efficiency and personal life if you are clear when it is time for you to put your tools down, or have time for personal life and family. Coinciding with the work hours of other colleagues at least some of the time is good sense. It means you can more easily collaborate, share tips, meet up in person and so on, and customers and clients will be reassured to know you are available for the work hours they keep.

Rameet Chawla of app development company Fueled (fueled.com) has his way: 'My overarching goal is to be consistent in my schedule, and as a result, I live a lifestyle that allows me to maximize the amount of work I get done. I believe this type of prioritization has made a huge impact on how quickly Fueled has grown.

'My dinner ends at 11 p.m., and I always have a solid work session afterwards until 3:30 a.m. Setting aside a block of time in my schedule for uninterrupted productive creation is vital to my work process. It's when I answer emails and do my thinking around bigger ideas without any distractions. Then I go to bed every day at exactly 4:00 a.m. and typically wake up without an alarm clock.

'Other people might want to focus on other areas, like family, but a consistent schedule is key.'

A work pattern to suit you

If you have this firmly in mind so that things do get done, then you can adapt how you work to a pattern that suits you. For instance I don't force myself to sit in my office, recording studio or wait ever ready for the phone to ring if it isn't necessary in order to complete my day's tasks. If we allow ourselves to see time out as a good thing, not least because evidence shows us that shorter, more focused hours can often be more productive than the long haul for the sake of it, then we benefit not just in terms of focusing better, but in reducing the stress that can accumulate so quickly in work life. I certainly find that if, for instance, I work extra hard four days of the week, I see no reason why I shouldn't take my wife away for a long weekend leaving all thoughts of earning streams at home.

Jonathan Self, a middle-aged writer, journalist and businessman, who has built up his different income streams to a point where he employs a team of people for the dog food business, and gets regular commissions for his writing, chooses to work limited hours and earn just enough to live on. For Jonathan, having time for the other things he wants to do tops greater riches and his past labours mean he has royalties coming in regularly from writing, so his basics are covered. He says:

'I choose to work a few hours a day to stay on top of things, but then I take a chunk of time in the middle of the day to have a leisurely lunch and read the papers. I might go for a walk for a couple of hours in the countryside around my home, and I do take holidays when it seems a good idea. The thing that worries me most is not being financially tighter than I am but wasting my time. And that is why I would hate paid employment. The people I know in office jobs talk about how much time is wasted.'

My mother, likewise, knows that she can be a bit relaxed about how she organises things these days, but she is clear that a structure you adhere to is very important when you first begin working as a solo entrepreneur. When she left *The Guardian*, and an imposed routine, she knew better than to listen to people who said cheerily she could go and have lunches and coffees with friends whenever she liked. Instead she made sure that the Monday after the farewell party, she was in her office at 9.30 a.m., and she made that her immutable rule for five days a week in which she also kept more or less to an eight hour day with a break at lunch time.

She explains: 'Working for myself, knowing I made the rules, it was very important to establish a work pattern that was realistic. Luckily I had commissions lined up so I just worked as though I were still employed. I've loosened up a bit through the years but I still regard Monday to Friday as working days. I think you have to be rigorous about keeping to the design for work that you have created for yourself.'

The late night worker

We all have 'biological clocks' of sorts that naturally tell us when the best time to work is. I like to wake up early because I find I'm more productive before the hustle and bustle of the city begins. But it is also when I feel my most refreshed, I find times are quiet so I can focus more and prevent the annoying sounds of midday traffic and noisy people bickering in the streets from creeping into my voice over recordings.

But not everyone is an early riser like myself. My friend Matt Harris is most definitely not a morning person and usually structures his day around working late and waking late as that works best for him. In conversations we've had, he tells me how he tends to wake up towards the middle of the day, goes for a walk in the park, has a coffee at his local café while reading up on the news, answering emails and writing musical ideas on a portable electronic device called a Korg Electribe that he'll later develop into fully fledged songs.

But it's during the late hours of the night that he feels he's most productive and when he gets most of his work done. That kind of timetable would have a boss from a 'regular job' up in arms, but it works for Matt and he's been very successful in a highly competitive industry, earning a lot more (he's reached over £70k on some years) than he would have if he'd chosen to stay in a 9-5 office job, and is based on his terms.

The limited structure

You might think Michael Bihovsky, with his clutch of LE jobs including actor and songwriter, recording engineer, musical arranger, director of theatre and film and composer of musical theatre, would need a very tightly organised structure. In fact he delights in being spontaneous much of the time. He explains:

'The only thing I structure is my student schedule, and to make sure that it leaves me with enough time to do my other work. It's only in the past year that I've figured out that if I schedule my students at random times throughout the week, it does not leave me with enough windows of time to get anything else done. I therefore now only teach on Mondays, Tuesdays, and Thursdays, and do my best to schedule all students on those days back-to-back. I have learned that if I only have an hour between students, I will not have time to do anything productive, and therefore I won't even try. If I cram all of my students into a few hours a day, however, I can use the rest of that day for other tasks.

'Regarding the other tasks, however, that is something that I rarely structure in advance. Whenever I find myself with extra time, I go over my mental or physical list of tasks that need to be done, and decide which I am most in the mood for at that particular moment. I find that if I am passionate about a particular project at a given moment, I will be much more productive than if I devote myself to something that I am not "feeling" at that time. Frequently I have to "bite the bullet" and work on something I don't want to, but the way I figure it, that's what most people have to do all the time.'

'I usually work on a few different things per day, but it depends on the nature of what I have to work on, and how much mental energy and time it will take to get done. I do tend to see projects through to their completion while I am working on them, and not spend the day switching back and forth. This allows me to enter a state of hyper-focus while I am working, which is my most productive state. I will usually have to check in on other projects or jobs on the same day, but I won't spend much time on them until I am done with whatever needs doing.'

'I absolutely believe that this shift in focus is what keeps me from going crazy. Precisely because I get so hyper-focused on whatever I am working on (no matter what it is), if that focus does not get dissipated on different subjects over time, I go a bit insane. This comes up most in website design, where the tasks are extremely arduous and monotonous. It's even worse when I have massive recording projects to engineer, as that can often lead to entire weeks where I am editing and mastering the same songs note by note, syllable by syllable, over and over and over again until I hear the sound of my brain breaking in half, only it turns out not to be my brain but my hard drive, losing me all of the work I have been doing every day for the past month (this has happened twice).'

Organising different jobs

If, as I do, you work on several rather different kinds of tasks, planning how best you can do this is especially important. If, for example, I have a particularly challenging website to create I know I need to keep my concentration absolutely focused on just that. So it is no good my thinking I'll "escape" the stress of trying to master a new form of coding, a new web language, by recording a couple of the voice-over commissions that have arrived on my desktop from *Fiverr*. On the other hand, when I have finished the web job I may make a bit of music for my own pleasure and as a way to 'come down' from the tension of getting the website to work as it should.

So you need to be very clear whether it benefits you to work on different income streams at the same time, scheduling say three hours for one and the same for the other two. This can work well if you have tasks that divide neatly into 'work bytes' - say you take on a three-hour childcare stint, then move on to writing a document that you have already roughed out so you can calculate the time it will take and finally you are making a set of embroidered cushions for a commission, you could finish the day with three hours doing this. I can see well how this would make for a day that is stimulating in its variety.

Suzanne Noble has been her own boss for too long to remember what it might be like to have one in charge of her, so she has worked out a fairly loose-limbed approach to her organisation, which relies on notebooks containing in minute detail what she must do each day, new ideas that come to her, telephone calls to be made, and so on. It is her support system and reassurance she has learnt to work on different tasks in one day by compartmentalising in her head. 'I will focus totally on what I am doing, but if say a phone call comes on a totally different subject, I am experienced enough to switch my focus to that, get the answer to a query, fix a meeting, take down the brief for a new commission and so on, then go back to what I was doing in the first place.'

Take a break

Another aspect of organisation, which is easy to overlook, is allowing break times when you get up from your desk, away from your table top, your research centre, the place you interview or deal with people. In the workplace breaks are accepted even if just 15 minutes for a cup of coffee or a stroll around to stretch the legs.

Working for yourself means you have to recognise the importance of these breaks to give a jaded brain a breathing space, to stretch limbs that can get very knotted if you are sitting all the time - I know people who slot in a ten-minute yoga or pilates session or a run around the block because they know they will come back to their tasks refreshed. I even have an alarm on my browser (Google Chrome) that allows me to set 30 minute 'blocks' so I can make sure I'm on track.

I've had quite a struggle telling myself that I don't have to do a full eight hours every day, most of us are so conditioned to believe we cannot be effective workers unless we do this. But the point of being a Lifestyle Entrepreneur is to learn that when it is not focused time or you are working for the sake of keeping yourself busy you would be far better doing something that engages you. Don't be afraid or ashamed to work fewer hours. Even if you end up doing just three hours on one day, but it's highly productive time and you know what you're doing is going to good use, then do that and don't let other people make you feel like you have to adhere to a conventional number of hours every day. Everyone is different and you'll know what kind of hours you need to put in as you build up your income streams.

9

KEEPING GOING

Having faith, hope and optimism when you get going is essential as well as, of course, enough funds to keep you afloat and a cool realism to see how you are going, to correct errors and see where there might be the need for some new aspect of your business to be introduced.

You need all the psychological buoyancy you can muster in the early days, when it's a waiting game to see if your idea really will hit the button. But once you are through that stage, and assuming you have made it to a place where you feel confident it is worth continuing and can see that it should be possible to make a sustainable income, you are into the business of keeping going.

This, then, is when you prepare for the long haul and work on adopting a mindset that will accommodate that idea. It is not the same thing as the first flush of excitement mixed with anxiety and nerves that marks the beginning stage. Now you have to have confidence that you are charting a path forward. You may already have sourced work and have clients, but if you have not got that far or have only put a toe in the water, then now is the time for dedicated action, a deep breath and to dive a little deeper.

Styled for success

It is common enough to see successful business folk's memoirs telling of years of graft to amass a fortune. American Sophie Amoruso, who can remember clearly the days she was going nowhere fast, a hitchhiking, dumpster-diving, community college dropout who, on whim, decided to have a shot at launching an online vintage clothes business from a pool hut . That was the genesis of Nasty Gal.

She was a one-woman band doing it all: merchandise, photographing, copywriting, and shipping items. She got up at the crack of dawn to get sorting merchandising, haggling with thrift stores and getting prices they gave reluctantly. She Photoshopped the images she styled and shot herself using models willing to back her idea. She described her process in an online interview.

'I'd grab an item and inspect to make sure it was in good shape. I'd zip zippers, button buttons, and hook hooks, then fold it and slide it into a clear plastic bag that I sealed with a sticker...Then I'd put it in a box and slap a shipping label on. Only I didn't slap anything - I took a lot of pride in how carefully I affixed those labels. I had to assume that my customer was as particular and as concerned with the aesthetics as I was.'

Her starting point had been a copy of *Starting an eBay Business for Dummies*, and her edgy styling and eye for cutting edge vintage brought a cult following of 60,000 fans to the website.

Eight years later, Nasty Gal has sold over $100 million in clothing and accessories both new and vintage. The business occupies a 65,000-square-foot office space in Los Angeles, employs over 350 people, and has over one million fans on Facebook and Instagram.

Not one to keep her business secrets to herself, Sophie published her book *Girl Boss* in 2014.

Brewing up a business

Andrew Birkby, one of the founders of *Wild Card Brewery*, describes how once they had their concept in place and had decided they would do all they could to make a go of the enterprise, they had to 'make some bold decisions.'

'The initial process was, we had about 200 pints of beer that we made at home...we were thinking about making a slightly different beer because our favourite beer is from a brewery in Nottingham.

Pale ales were all over the place in London and we thought ok let's do something about this. We spent 2 years in arriving at the perfect recipe. We decided this is the one and we are good to go. All in various bottles with logos and everything. There were some 5 or 6 sales to start with. We secured some good sales early on, prospectively, with a promise to deliver in a month or two. We took his credit card, and we bought the ingredients, hired equipment for a day and made beer to fulfil all the orders. We also had some stockpile. We did some door-to-door sales etc. It became a routine pretty soon.'

William takes over explaining, 'Basically we learnt a lot from textbooks. You just need to read a lot and practice at home. The recipe for the beer Jack of Clubs started out in a beer forum years and years ago. The recipe we originally started with was all crystal malt which gives a dark beer. We wanted a much easier-to-drink beer which still had all the flavour and the colour. So we tweaked it for 2 years by changing the ratios until we were satisfied.'

You may have realised by this time that being a Lifestyle Entrepreneur is not for most people a magic formula which brings a quick financial kill and lots of free time, especially if you're in a competitive industry or your interests are in a particularly niche area. You may, as many of us hope, reach a point where you earn enough with a moderate number of work hours per day, and a happy healthy balance with private life, but be prepared to work hard if you are building up an enterprise.

And if you are going the multi-stream way, you may find hours you would never have contemplated in an office, but this is the way it has to be. I certainly do sixteen-hour days when all my earning strands are bringing in work that needs doing to a deadline, but because I have chosen this way and know I can, equally, if there is a quiet patch, take a few leisurely days, it doesn't feel oppressive or unreasonable.

Surprise success

It was serendipity coming across the marketplace Fiverr. I spotted a section for voice-over recordings, tried setting up a couple of gigs, and it has become a significant earning stream ever since. It's great to know that I can now only do web jobs that seem worthwhile and interest me as I don't rely on them financially and that is largely in part due to the surprise success of my work on Fiverr.

In the UK, People per Hour works in a similar way to Fiverr and, although I've not really pushed to get much work there as I decided to focus on music which is harder to earn from there, the brief period I was on the site yielded a few jobs and contacts who I continue to work with today.

The great thing about platforms like Fiverr and People per Hour, which trade in services, is that you neither have to commit yourself to a particular amount of time, nor invest any money unless you want to. You take on jobs as they come and if you want, which means you can limit the time you give them. For example, if I have a particularly challenging piece of music to create, I turn off gigs on Fiverr until I am finished, then switch it on again when I'm ready.

Try out prices

As with crowdfunding sites, another advantage is that sites like these get a lot of traffic which makes them good places to try out your product and see whether it is something that the market demands. They are a good place to test the market for what sells and what you can charge.

On the whole people go to them as a cheaper way of getting what they want than from conventional traders or companies offering, say, translation or language teaching which are among the many services to be found on People per Hour and Fiverr. It's not the only way of trading as an individual but it's a lot more time effective than putting leaflets through doors or cold-calling - although cold-calling, if you are very good at establishing contact on the phone so that people want to listen to you, may build a more enduring client-customer relationship. Just avoid those deadly scripts that so many callers are clearly given, and which they recite in a way that suggests they are less than enthused.

Confidence in failure

However you do it, putting yourself out there can be daunting in the beginning, and it can be tough on the ego if you get too many rejections. Rather than feeling useless, helpless, and not wanting to risk more, we need to adopt the American idea that what we call failure is actually a learning curve. The popular attitude in the US is to try something out and when it doesn't work out, they consider it an indication that they need to try something new, a different way.

I've tried hard to adopt this way of thinking when, for example, I have uploaded my music to some of the marketplaces that take on tracks they think are good enough and allow you to sell them on their platform. But there have been a number that just don't move, nobody is interested in or don't receive any views at all, and it is very easy to get depressed. Yet it is far better instead to ask yourself why your product is not selling, through constructive questions like:

- Is the quality of my work up to scratch in comparison to the competition?
- Is anybody actually *finding* my work? I.e. do I need to change my description / tags / marketing techniques?
- Is the market already saturated with what I'm offering?
- Is it clear the return on investment people will get from my work?
- Are my prices too high or too low (if the marketplace lets you set your own price)?

Maybe you need to change your style or content to see whether people respond better to something different. Maybe you need to bring in new ingredients, as I have done recently by working with a Spanish Flamenco guitarist on a Flamenco-fusion album for a music library that lacked that style of music in its repertoire (and is sought after by clients according to the library owner). In the same vein, in 2014 I did a Tango breakbeat album for the same library because I saw a niche opportunity there based on about an hour's research looking at what was already out there.

If you are not getting the response that you expected (or want), do a bit of marketing, use social media to try to familiarise yourself with the names of people who have an interest in what you are offering, and ask them directly, as I did with the library, what they are looking for. There's nothing better than getting that info straight from the horse's mouth.

Business leads

Getting new business is something that is always worth planning for. It is the key to having more work lined up. Creating business opportunities might seem like a daunting task at first but, as with social media, starting a dialogue with potential clients in a casual and friendly conversational manner is a far better way than the hard sales approach. Try reaching out to people in a non-salesy way and you'll likely fare better as people will not have their 'sales-guard' up.

I've often got future business leads from the marketplaces I trade on as customers have put me in touch with other companies through word-of-mouth or, following a business transaction, the client and I will have established an ongoing working relationship. Many of my orders on Fiverr are repeat customers for example, and indeed return customers are the staple for a steady stream of work. So, marketplaces can be a good source for generating your own leads as well as the work itself.

Build a contact list

Build a contact list as return customers are the staple for a steady stream of work. Contacts leads to making money and Internet marketers often use the saying 'the money is in the list' to stress how building up a targeted email list with a list-building strategy will let you market to your customers directly, which can lead to sales. The larger the list, and the better your strategy, the more likely you'll get a bunch of sales.

And if you think about it, it makes sense. Having a system for collecting and storing your new and old contacts who are interested in what you're offering means you have a 'sales' list with whom you can contact easily. You can begin building a relationship with them and convert them to customers, just make sure you cater your communications to their needs and don't spam them with too many messages so they hang around.

For instance, my mother says she lists people interviewed with a brief description of what the interview was about and for whom she wrote it, along with a telephone number, email and address. This acts as a database of potential interviewees she can refer to if she has further ideas to pitch to newspapers, magazines, book editors etc.

It might seem easy to keep this kind of database on your computer, but it is definitely worth keeping a hard copy or a backup on a third-party service like Google Drive or Dropbox as well, as most of us have computer problems at some time like a crash, a virus destroying your hard drive, or a cat deciding to coat your laptop in coffee with a nonchalant flick of its tail. If you don't have a backup, you can lose all that data or cannot get on with work for many hours, which of course is very bad news.

Collect emails

Collecting email addresses - building an email 'list' - is essential as it gives you a quick and economical way of contacting your customers to inform them, for instance, about something new you are doing.

I have an email list for my website contacts and am in the process of building up an email list for my music via Instrumental Background Music, a website I built to sell my royalty-free music directly. As a shameless plug, you can sign up and get a free track to use in your video / podcast / other marketing material here:

www.instrumentalbackgroundmusic.com.

Here are some tips for building an email list from scratch:

- Use ads (such as from Facebook, Reddit or Google) to drive traffic to a landing page where people can sign up for something, whether it is news, a free download or a discount.
- Hold contests and announce freebies on social media networks.
- Include a sign up form in the header (top part) and footer (bottom area) of your site so it's easy for people to sign up.
- 'Cold-email' clients asking them if they'd like to be part of a VIP list (make sure it's actually VIP!) on industry news or offers.
- Get your friends to promote a landing page through their social accounts (being endorsed by friends is an effective way of gaining people's trust online).
- Ask people to sign up in any videos and other content you publish online. For example, if you 'vlog' on YouTube, ask people to sign up to your mailing list to be notified when a new video is out.
- Run holiday or seasonal promotions to get people to sign up.

A few places you can use to collect email addresses for free (and in some cases even send emails to your customers) are Mailchimp, Campaign Monitor and SignUpAnywhere. Just remember to occasionally export the contacts you collect and save them in a safe place!

One last point regarding collecting contact details is that if you handle personal information, you may need to register as a data controller with the ICO (ico.org.uk/for-organisations/business).

Buy in help

Of course, if you're building a list, remember that you need to produce content that will make people *want* to stay subscribed. All the work in building a list can easily be undone if you don't deliver on the promise you sold the subscriber when they signed up.

And if you're thinking it's a lot of work producing this content, then you could be right! But it doesn't mean *you* have to do it, nor that you need to do it all in one go. Automating the process through things like scheduling emails that drip-feed content over the course of a year and outsourcing to places such as *Upwork*, People per Hour and Fiverr to write your copy for you, proofread, design a logo or website, and so on, are popular ways to free up your time.

Outsourcing

When you buy in labour like this it is known as outsourcing, and a great many Lifestyle Entrepreneurs do it. One of the benefits is that you may find someone who can work with you regularly and may even become a friend, or you may tap into a network of people who want to collaborate on a project and bring you in.

It can be a lot of work building multiple streams of income, so rather than panicking, finding yourself working insane hours, feeling forever stressed etc. it can make absolute sense to buy in services from outside that other people offer. As mentioned, there are various places online you can find people to hire based in countries around the globe.

On the trading sites such as those described, people from a huge variety of countries with very different skills offer their services. Finding out who is good, who is worth what they charge and so on is, of course, a matter of trial and error and vetting people properly with questions that are relevant to the work / role, checking their credentials etc. Something I've done in the past is give someone a small test job before I trust them with an important project.

For example, I'm not that fond of data entry, which is an important part of the upload process when selling music online as the 'meta data', as it's known (things like descriptions, tags, titles and tempo info), is what people use to find your music. The work is laborious, takes time and is a special kind of boring, so I outsourced it all to someone on *Upwork* after giving them a small sample as a test. It took about a day to upload all the tracks for each library and meta-tag them etc., but it was well worth getting someone else involved to liberate me from the unbelievable boredom of doing it myself (plus the potential repetitive strain injury that comes with doing the same thing over and over and over again).

Things don't always go smoothly of course, but that is why you should vet the people you work with, value those who are good, and develop long-lasting relationships with the really special ones, as they can be your life line in difficult times when time is short. I've had a few instances where I've tried to get some SEO work done and the results have been appalling. I was partly to blame because if something is too good to be true, it probably is, and I was wooed on price, but bear in mind that sometimes a little patience is required to find good providers.

And there are plenty of situations when you might need or just choose to outsource some work. My mother regularly gets her interviews transcribed, I've employed people to fill up online shops I've built with large numbers of products, I have friends who have had logos designed, got voice-overs done on their videos, and leaflets designed and printed, among all sorts of other things. A director whose films I score has a virtual assistant in India to help him run tasks for his film work and businesses.

Outsourcing really can be a worthwhile investment, and even an economy, if you are likely to fail to meet a deadline or have things to do that prevent you from being able to complete your work on time, for example. And by outsourcing, you're often helping another LE to survive, thereby building up the culture of being a solo entrepreneur within which we can support each other.

Things to Consider

If you require a document in perfect prose and with impeccable grammar it is probably best to get someone in your mother tongue and with an education suitable for the task. If you are hiring in someone to do cold-calling, for example, you'll want them to speak your language fluently.

And, as with all outsourcing, you should look at whether you will earn more than you're going to spend for a job so you're not out of pocket. When I outsourced the meta-tagging and uploading of all my music to various online music libraries, not only will the sales of my music repay those costs over times many times over, I actually earned twice the amount by doing some web work using the time I'd freed up, so it really was a no brainer investment.

Lastly, it helps to be clear when hiring in someone about what you're looking for, your budget, how long you intend to hire them for, and come to an agreement about how many revisions to the work is reasonable.

Choosing who to hire

John Greathouse, who teaches courses on entrepreneurship at the University of California at Santa Barbara, believes you should always look to hire people locally rather than remotely because:

- They are easier to find and to check references.
- You can gain access to other talent in their network if you need it.
- It's more likely you'll find someone who 'fits' in better as you share cultural values.
- There's less risk of them needing to relocate if you require them regularly.

And obviously if you need someone to prepare a product for you in person, to be able to come to your home to sort out filing, work on your computer and so on, you need to find someone based reasonably close.

Strict vetting

My experience is that hiring in remotely doesn't need to be risky if you investigate who you're hiring beforehand. On many sites like

Upwork, Elance and *Freelancer* there are already strict vetting procedures in place for sellers, guides on how to choose a seller, and incentives for sellers to maintain a good standing in the marketplace. Online ratings, comments, credentials and experience are all useful indicators of whether someone is likely to deliver quality work on time or not.

You can also use these trading sites to offer your own services or advertise locally, but bear in mind that everything we've talked about above will influence how much work you'll receive as well. The better you come across and the higher the quality of work and value you deliver, the greater your chances of maintaining a steady stream of income will be.

Up your game

It is particularly important in the music industry – but really in any branch of business - to continually improve your work as the bar is being raised every day. The technology and tools used to make music has become ever cheaper (even free) meaning the quality of goods is not only higher than before, but the markets are becoming saturated as more people upload music and can make it faster. It has meant I've needed to adapt and improve my music and production skills to compete.

This is something you'll most likely need to do too, but it is a positive thing. As well as opening up new avenues for earning, it can be invigorating to improve your skills and learn new techniques, and the more you do it, the further it sets you apart from the competition.

Start by asking yourself if you're offering something that is *better* than what's already out there. If you're honest with yourself and you're not as good as the competition, ask yourself why, what you can do to reach that point, and maybe even consider trying a different product or service if the current one isn't getting much luck. If you can demonstrate *why* you are better than those trying to do the same thing as you, you're on the right track.

You might offer something different, improved or more

competitive in terms of price, design or functionality. Or something that's just more innovative than what is out there. But at the end of the day, it really is about offering the *best value* and being aware of changes in the marketplace (such as what is currently hot) to keep business coming.

Quality not quantity

Offering the 'best value' does not necessarily mean you are offering the 'most product' or 'most time' in your service, it can mean that you're offering something that is hard to find elsewhere because of its particularly high quality. What people perceive as high quality is also just as important - I am very clear that I'm not the cheapest option people will find out there when doing voice-over work, but because I am confident in the quality of my recordings, have a strong portfolio to back me up, and lots of positive feedback from customers, people perceive my work as good quality and I can charge more than the rest.

Using music as an example, there are countless people out there filling up marketplaces like AudioJungle with songs that are of average quality. Yet if you look at the top sellers on many market-places, you'll see many of them selling far more than the competition with tiny portfolios because they have focused on creating high quality music that is very usable. And if they don't have small portfolios, it's often only a handful of their items that sell well.

Of course, even top authors have to do some marketing, which we'll cover in a later chapter, but offering the highest quality you can will make you stand out among the crowd and bring in more business in an overcrowded market.

Joining forces with other businesses

Can the competition become an ally? Promoting your competitors when you can't deliver - and this is assuming you consider them good at what they do - can be an effective way of keeping customers coming back to you in the future.

I've had to pass on work when I've been too busy or am asked to do something beyond my skill set. But by becoming a trusted source for *solving their problems*, my clients often come back to me first if they have a job rather than the competition I referred them to. At the end of the day, sustainable businesses are all about relationships.

Obviously this comes with a caveat, as not everyone is interested in sharing their clientele. But by being a good neighbour to surrounding businesses, you build a bigger network, which means more work can come your way.

Getting your money

If you are used to receiving a regular pay packet and not having to think about what is entailed in getting paid, it can come as a bit of a jolt to find, once you are a lone operator, people may not pay invoices on time, may not pay them at all, may query what you have done as a delaying tactic or a way of blaming you for the fact you are not getting paid.

Dealing with this kind of behaviour is not pleasant and it is time-consuming, but you need to develop a tough approach, because if you don't, you may end up very broke and with your business down the tube. That said, most people do pay honourably and fairly promptly, but if they don't you need to have a strategy in mind. David Nicholson says:

'Sometimes I have rows with people if they hint that they are not happy to pay or if they rescind commissions when I have started work. One magazine rescinded a commission when I had been working on the project for two weeks. They were intractable about this and there was no question of even a kill fee so I sued and they settled. Sometimes, even if it feels risky, you have to look after yourself. I'm not prepared to be treated that way. It is about valuing oneself, not feeling you are just one of so many freelancers out there and therefore anybody else will do. But I burnt my bridges with that company.'

The *Wild Card Brewery* have also had troubles with getting paid, as Andrew says:

'Probably the most difficult thing is getting paid and chasing invoices. Many times we deliver the goods but don't get paid. At first there was a lot of hand wringing over what to do but generally we find the best way is to ring the customer as often as necessary, or go and speak to them in person. People may shout at you, but you have to swallow it and move on. Or you get the line that they haven't been paid and therefore can't pay us.

'The big drawback for small companies is that they don't have the kind of fat bank accounts that big companies do where if people owe you and you owe them, there is a cushion to fall back on.'

As I write this, I've had to quickly prepare a bunch of invoices for a couple of the active income streams I've set up. You should factor this kind of work into your plan as a multi-stream earner, as it takes up time yet is essential in order to get paid. And while I tend to put together my invoices by hand because I like to brand myself in detail, there are services like *Freshbooks* (freshbooks.com) that will make your life a lot easier when it comes to invoicing, tracking time, and reminding clients to pay.

If you trade through a website like *Upwork* or *Elance*, then bear in mind that they pay you through their own payment system and often don't clear the money right away. Many times I've needed to wait a month for my music earnings to come through or a couple of weeks for voice-over work to clear, so factor this into how you plan your spending.

While it may be tempting (and satisfying) to watch your earnings accumulate, the sooner you get your earnings into your hands, the better. Martin Lewis makes a good point on his website MoneySavingExpert.com:

'Don't store cash in online-earning accounts. These companies aren't banks. There's no protection if one closes, taking your cash with it. So withdraw your cash as soon as you reach the payment threshold.'

Remember, the longer your money is in another person's hands, the harder it could become to get it back.

Safeguard yourself

You'll inevitably come up against clients who, for one reason or another, don't pay on time. There are many schools of thought on how to avoid awkward moments like this, such as:

- Charging everything up front, especially for clients you've never worked with before.
- Getting 50% up front and the remainder on delivery.
- Asking for 30% at the start, 30% on delivery of a demo and 40% on final delivery.
- Trusting your client and just invoice at the end.

How you ask for payment should really depend on your relationship with the client, as no two are the same. I switch between options 3 and 4 quite often, but have asked for 50% up front before if I feel uneasy with the person for whom I am working, or I have no history with them.

If you're having trouble getting paid for a job, it is always best to start with gentle reminders and keeping in close contact with the client or their accounts department. If reasonable negotiations fail, you can always take the issue to a small claims court, however, bear in mind this can be a long and time-consuming process.

What you do is more than what you earn is the thing

It is exciting to find such enthusiasm for social enterprise, not from a bleeding hearts' perspective so much as a great enthusiasm for the idea that it is possible to be an agent of change, even if you don't have Bill Gates kinds of funds to spend, or a raft of celebrities putting their name to your enterprise. There are people who are not motivated simply by making a great deal of money, but also by feeling good with who and what they are in the world.

We are not talking sentimentality here: of the social entrepreneurs we have interviewed, all recognise they need to make a living, and that having enough money to live comfortably, without the stress and insecurity that real poverty brings, is what they want. But that is very different to the drive that seemed to be programmed into so many of the young from very early years - I even came across a website offering guidance on priming your child to be a future entrepreneur - and that success was primarily having a position of recognised status and earnings that would rise steadily.

There is realism too that cutting loose from convention to create this lifestyle may mean living on the most basic income to grow enterprises. I am full of admiration for people like David Floyd, who has kept going with considerable success, running an award winning social innovation organisation *Social Spider*.

David founded the company in 2003 and was joined by Mark Brown. They support, research and write about social enterprise and social innovation. In 2013 *Social Spider* won the Future 50 Young Entrepreneurs Award for 'entrepreneurial flair and innovation in running a responsible business venture.' David says 'In the world of social enterprise we are quite an unusual organisation. We've been involved in a huge range of stuff over the years, some successful, some less so, but all a good learning experience.'

And if we are talking heart rather than hard commerce as the driving force in enterprise, how cheering to hear that *Social Spider* has been commissioned to research and write a report exploring the role of love in social enterprise, based on interviews with some of the UK's leading social entrepreneurs. As well as a project asking people all across England who have (or have had) mental health difficulties to record a day in their lives once a season, analysing what they share.

Alongside his role with *Social Spider*, David is non-executive director of *Significant Seams CIC* (significantseams.org.uk), a social enterprise that nurtures self-confidence and community through textile crafts and traditions, and *Impress* (inpressbooks.co.uk), the sales and marketing agency for independent publishers in the UK. He is a member of the governing council of *Social Enterprise UK* and a fellow of the *RSA* and the *School for Social Entrepreneurs*. Oh and there is, from time to time, a poetry performance.

Add to this a vigorous public voice to be heard on his blog *Beanbags and Bullshit* where, among other things, he critiques the inadequacies of thinking about the role of social innovation as resting on 'an explosion of Ashoka-model, Richard Branson-style heroic social entrepreneurs. Let's get real', he says, 'no heroic social entrepreneurs at all have solved a global social problem (or even replaced a relatively small existing public service) by scaling up themselves and doing their passion.'

Yet his passion is the reason he chooses a lifestyle that involves him with the possibility of playing his part in social change. He puts it this way: 'Mark and I have particular ideas about how we'd like the world to change and what we'd like to see happen, but we are not trying to solve one thing. We don't have a specific mission.'

10

THE MONEY STUFF

You have probably heard of the gabby entrepreneurs who boast online of the fortunes they have made by selling a couple of bright ideas and on how you too can become rich. And, they assure us, if we put in the sweat and tears necessary we too can get there. Some even suggest we may be able become mega rich without having to work too many hours at all.

Oh and let's not forget: most have a manual, a book, a set of seminars and so on you need to purchase in order to learn the knack.

The get-rich-quick notion

Even though we see these online gurus frequently fuelling the dream that with their guidance you can amass riches enough to make The Wolf of Wall Street feel impoverished, they should be regarded with scepticism. More on that later, but equally significant in my view is that my research found a great many people happy to live on a modest income because it gives them the *lifestyle* they want, and for whom the gurus promising what may be a Mephistophelian deal are not enticing.

What I am seeing in the LE is a desire to organise a life that capitalises on their personal abilities and talents, rather than a one-size-fits-all system. They want a way of earning and living that has the human touch. Something that is less focused on making a lot of money as the universal goal and more concerned with a well-balanced life within which work is a rewarding ingredient.

That said, I do not believe in dismissing anything until I have attempted to know more. So I asked Andrew Warner, who started Mixergy - a website that he describes is a place for the ambitious to learn from a mix of experienced mentors through interviews and courses - to tell me. He introduces himself online this way:

'Hi, I'm Andrew Warner. In my 20s, I used credit cards and ingenuity to create a $30-plus million a year (in sales) Internet business with my younger brother. The Mixergy Mission is to introduce you to doers and thinkers whose ideas and stories are so powerful that just hearing them will change you.'

So I approached Andrew for an interview, wanting to understand more about how he works. He thanked me, told me he was flattered and that I should fix a time. However, before my allotted time came, and after I had sent a list of questions, I received an email saying he didn't have time to do an interview. I then heard that someone else I know had exactly the same experience. Since then, I have been bombarded with promotional Mixergy material, but no enlightenment.

And that's not just me. I can name others who have had precisely the same experience: the apparent desire to talk to an interested individual who is then offered the chance to book a time slot when he will call you. It quite warms the heart, this willingness to engage so personally. Except that the willingness doesn't materialise, so that all the hyperbolic testimonials on Warner's webpage are presumably from people who have signed on for what Mixergy offers rather than wanting an informative one-to-one chat with Andrew.

I am not alone in thinking it wise to be wary of these get-rich-quick promises. A highly critical article in *The Daily Telegraph* referred to 'a sprawling unregulated industry that offers to help ordinary people start online enterprises and make money.' A trawl through the online world of people calling themselves entrepreneurs offering virtually failsafe routes to big-league money-making that only they can help you reach.

Jason Jones, who runs the site *Salty Droid*, which takes an askance look at such enterprises, is quoted saying that Internet money-making is the great delusion of our time, that the whole Internet marketing industry plays on people's ignorance. The lure is often a webinar or eBook as a hook in to get you buying seminars and months-long mentoring programmes that can cost thousands of pounds.

One of his caution-urging blogs puts it this way: 'You can use the Internet to help you sell goods or services but as it was before the Internet, your success or failure will depend mostly on the quality or cost of your stuffs; on your ability to attract the attention of the marketplace - and on plain dumb luck. The Internet as an automated success machine is just a mean lie.'

There is also a warning from the Wikipedia website pointing out that get-rich-quick schemes operating solely on the Internet promote themselves as offering some mysterious secret they can impart to affiliate marketing and affiliate advertising. A tantalising near-promise of quickly earned, high sums is generally the bottom line. The carrot being that you will earn far more than you pay out to learn the advertiser's method. Yet as plenty have found when they do succumb to this temptation, what they receive as training for success is material that is often straightforward marketing techniques, which can often be found with a good online search of your own.

The tricksy, beguiling bit is that these online marketing 'gurus' display testimonials from 'previous users,' that talk of enriching transformations. And a warning is that when you try to navigate away from one of these websites, users are often presented with pop-up windows offering further discounts, perhaps in an attempt to make them feel special, or to seem too good to resist any further.

On the other hand Trent Hamm, who lives in Des Moines with his wife and young children, did not set out to make money but rather took the standpoint of a zealot who wanted to tell the world how much better his life was once he learned to handle finances in a way that bought him freedom.

He came to *The Simple Dollar* project, his philosophy for earning as a LE, motivated by a determination to get out of the large debt he had amassed by living carelessly, a lifestyle that had him caught in a highly paid but also highly demanding job, leaving little family time. The birth of his first child was a wake-up call, and he has described the surge of love and urgency that cradling his newborn baby brought.

Trent began with *The Simple Dollar* website on which he writes two blog posts a day about financial self improvement, not being a slave to making money, and ways to be frugal without living in a hair-shirt. He has written two books on his approaches to money and been successful enough with his multi-stream earning lifestyle to give up the well-paid job that acted as a launch pad for his determination to build a different lifestyle. *The Simple Dollar* has been enough of a success for him to be featured in *Time magazine* and the *Financial Times*.

His books have attracted great enthusiasm and considerable criticism, but enough people have wanted to read them, as well as him having hundreds of thousands of followers on his blog, that today he is a wealthy man. He sees it this way, he told *Time Magazine*:

'It's a lot easier to trust the advice of someone who made a disaster of things and fixed it themselves than someone who has never been through that Mephistophelian deal in the first place,' and, he adds with evident satisfaction, 'I make significantly more than I spend, so I can pay off debts and eventually build up more sources of passive income.'

But you may get rich

Getting rich is, of course, possible and within the LE world you see people who have had a lightbulb moment and created something that has just taken off. There are also people who get rich by pursuing what interests them with no notion where it may lead but travelling hopefully. Yet, as Alyson Shontell on *Business Insider* online sagely tells us for entrepreneurs, one good idea can provide an extraordinary amount of hope. She puts it this way:

'Even though the chances of success are minimal, these ideas give people something to aspire to greater than a boring cubicle and a nagging boss. Not to mention, these ideas make some people obscenely loaded. If you're waiting to act on one of these ideas until you think of something brilliant, don't.'

She gives some wonderfully wacky examples of how ideas that would surely be laughed out of town have in fact hit riches. Take Charlie Ball, whose story Shontell relates with gusto:

'Back in 1963 his father, Harvey, first drew the happy face for his PR company's client, State Mutual Life Insurance. The only money the Balls ever made from the simple sketch was the two-figure dollar amount they made selling it to the client.

'So who did make all that money off the brilliantly simple symbol? Two brothers, Bernard and Murray Spain, stumbled upon the unrealized potential of the smiley. Wanting to start a novelty store, Bernard and Murray bought the legal rights to the mark along with the now infamous tag-line, "Have a nice day."'

The brothers' approach was to use the image everywhere and anywhere they could. The yellow smiley took off and was suddenly being used for every kind of product and promotion. The fad peaked in 1971 and diminished after a year and a half, Shontell says, but that was enough time to net $50 million in sales. Fired with their entrepreneurial success, the brothers opened the first *Dollar Express* in the US in the 1980s and they continued to sell the smiley. In 2000 they sold their chain to *Dollar Tree* for $500 million.

Nicko Williamson, who wrote a business plan for his eco-friendly taxi service, while still at university, is now making millions. In 2007, having raised £200,000 from family and friends and an additional £300,000 through an Angel network, Nicko founded Climatecars. Today, his taxis cover the whole of Greater London, and have 650 companies as clients. He has reached annual turnover of £3 million, according to BusinessGreen, which awarded him Young Sustainability Executive of the Year in 2011.

Dream it, do it

Then there is Jamal Edwards, a multi-millionaire at 24, who tells an engaging story of being an estate school kid who saw that having GCSEs and degrees didn't seem to get his mates far, and so he decided that was not for him. Instead he found a way that has made him a multi-millionaire. He has been described as the smartest operator and self-promoter in town, and on his Twitter feed he poses the brash question (which is also a quote from George Bernard Shaw):

'There are those who look at things and ask why. I'd say dream of things that never were and ask why not?'

Aged 15, he began amateur film-making around his estate after his parents gave him a basic video camera as a gift. This he did in his spare time while working in a shop after school. He put some of his films on YouTube. Neighbours and mates with showbiz aspirations began to ask him to film and post them. He gained enough of a reputation for the way his films portrayed up and coming stars that his hits grew rapidly, advertising came in, and he could do it full time.

That was then, and just eleven years later he is the media boss who founded SBTV, a broadcasting company that makes videos mostly featuring rap and pop music stars, and still puts them on YouTube.

Jamal attracts millions of hits and the business continues to make a fortune by taking a percentage of YouTube's advertising revenues for adverts that are linked to its videos. He has featured on the *Sunday Times Rich List*, and is not offering a magic formula for us to follow. What he has done is entirely idiosyncratic, but he does have a line in philosophical thinking: 'Try anything, don't be scared of failure, that is my advice. The only failure is not trying.'

Interviewed recently, he was reflective about what success means for him: 'By following my passion, I've been able to fly around the world. I've been on tour with Dr Dre and Rihanna and been invited to meet Bill Gates in Seattle. Then, I've got friends who've been to university and are struggling to get jobs - that's mad. This didn't happen because of my GCSEs or where I came from. Anyone can be a success on YouTube just as long as they have a good idea and know how to capitalise on it.'

Overheads and accounts

Good with numbers and got top marks in maths? Maybe doing your own accounts makes sense to you, but bear in mind that if your multi-stream income suddenly becomes popular, or if you have many streams of income, it could be wise to invest in an accountant and a bookkeeper so you can focus on the things that you enjoy or simply free up your time.

Regardless of whether you hire someone else for your accounting, be meticulous about keeping receipts and any proof of spending that is work-related. Create a system that works for you and that you will find simple to keep up with.

For instance, I photograph receipts with my phone and send them to myself so I can organise them efficiently along with other electronic receipts. And phone apps like *Fresh Xpense Capture* for the iPhone exist especially for this purpose. If you're on Android, *Smart Receipts* is considered a good alternative, although many more exist if you do a search.

To keep track of your earnings, it might be worth creating a spreadsheet where you record your income and outgoings. I do this using a spreadsheet hosted in Google Drive so I can access it via the net wherever I am in the world.

Legalities

Finally, you should be aware of the legalities of how you make your income, particularly if you're dealing with clients in different parts of the world. In many cases, the rules and regulations of where you are domicile / resident take effect, but if in doubt, always ask an expert like a business lawyer.

For example, if you outsource to someone who works as a freelancer / independent contractor, then the taxes and laws often become less complex. You are essentially doing a 'work for hire' contract where you don't need to pay social security, holiday or sick leave as you would a full-time employee.

Government websites like www.gov.uk/business provide useful information on the legal side of running a business or acting as a sole trader, and you can also call your local tax office, who should offer some guidance.

Taxes

If you are a LE, you cannot afford to be casual about your tax. I can point you to several people working on their own projects who simply didn't bother with tax for a few years and found they were landed with bills that would gobble up any profits for years to come.

It is worth heeding Trent Hamm of *The Simple Dollar's* advice when he suggests putting aside 50% of your earnings for tax, National Insurance, and any unexpected expenses that come up.

Although I consider myself decent with numbers, I employ an accountant to help make sure my accounts are kept in order and I pay the right amount of tax. In the UK, there is also a VAT earnings threshold over which you must register for and pay VAT, so keep an eye on your earnings to make sure you are doing your accounts properly as you want to avoid suddenly having to take 20% or so off your earnings or surprising your clients with a sudden hike in prices due to needing to add VAT.

Some other things to think about are:

- When do your taxes need to be paid by? Make sure you don't miss the deadline!
- Have you factored taxes into your prices so you are actually making enough to survive on / make a profit?
- Are you clear about what is and isn't considered an expense? Call your tax authority if in doubt.
- Can you outsource any part of the process you're having trouble with, like bookkeeping?
- Are there any regional taxes you need to take into consideration when selling?
- If you're selling digital goods to the EU, make sure you look into EU VAT and if it affects you (euvataction.org).

By having a clear roadmap of how you're going to deal with taxes and making sure you're covering yourself as you go along, you'll have significant peace of mind and far fewer surprises when it comes to paying your taxes and counting your profits.

11

THE INTEGRATED LIFE

I had the perfect weekend planned - a leisurely day on the beach with my new wife, whom I hadn't seen for a week, as I had been in London meeting clients and organising projects.

Then a meal with her family and an evening hanging together watching a film, chatting, and wondering about visiting friends the next day.

That was the plan. The reality was very different. The moment I arrived in Spain and checked my emails there were requests from three of the companies I work for online asking if I could do some emergency work for them. I had more orders than ever for the voice-over service I put up on Fiverr a few weeks ago, and one of the libraries I sell to wanted extra tracks for an album I was creating for them. Oh, and I had a couple of chapters of this book to get written.

Obviously, being in demand when you work for yourself is welcome, and much of my time is spent making sure I am marketing myself properly and drawing in new business. But occasions like the weekend I was so looking forward to can all too easily be victims of the thing that anyone who works for themselves probably knows - keeping clients happy is all important.

So my plans with my wife had to be trimmed to an afternoon on the beach and no visit to friends the next day. Fortunately she understands that if I am going to work for myself and have the advantages of flexible time, with the possibility of taking an impromptu break, sometimes there is sacrifice. But even so, it felt disappointing.

I remember my mother, when I was young, would be perched in the garden with the electric typewriter she had before computers became commonplace, tapping out an article for a frantic deadline, sketching the outline for a new book, or planning a journalism lecture, on a Saturday afternoon when I wanted her and my Dad, also often busy with his work projects, to do something all together as a family. But much more often they would make the time for my brother and me at weekends, and to collect us from school, give us tea, do the bedtime routine, even if it meant my Dad sitting up half the night doing accounts and my Mum writing articles until the early hours.

One of the reasons people choose to become their own boss is the idea that creating their own pattern of work and destiny is far more compatible with having a private life, a family life, than a waged life in the Western world enables, where the hours you are expected to devote to your employer, rather than loved ones and friends, all too often extend beyond the traditional eight-hour day (particularly if you want to be seen as keen and marked for promotion).

Vicky Ward in *Devil's Casino*, her entertaining exploration of the life of employees of the Lehman Brothers before their collapse, described the price of the luxurious lifestyle she and her family could have at the loss of any right to expect some home life with her husband. If the boss wanted him at a Christmas day cocktail party there was no arguing; should she be having a baby and there was a board meeting scheduled, forget it. The happy idea of the future Dad being there with you and so on was out of the question.

Or, if you have a less prestigious salaried job, insecurity may lurk like a malign ghost threatening to reduce your hours at any time, be laid off, or have shifts inconveniently altered. You have no control over any of these, yet all have a damaging effect on your home and social life. Nor do you have the possibility of carving out a compensatory chunk of time for family and friends when the kind of sudden must-do work, which appeared on my planned recreational weekend, occurs. As an employee, you are not in control of the steering wheel.

Martina Mercer does copywriting and journalism blogging at People per Hour, the online employment marketplace. She understands well the underlying anxiety that makes it very hard to risk missing an opportunity, to take on everything offered in case there is a sudden work drought, feeling you must be available for clients at any time. It can too easily mean there is little time left over for the other part of life, as she describes:

'When you own your own business or are a freelancer, managing your work-life balance is not as easy as it seems. It's ironic that many of us choose this career path for the flexibility and freedom yet end up working more hours than those in average nine to five hours.'

Trent Hamm, who set up *The Simple Dollar* project that we mentioned earlier, prefers cooking at his Des Moines home with his wife and young children to visiting fashionable restaurants and being on the town. Like many LEs, as his time has become his own to organise, he can relax enough to enjoy domesticity in a way that can be far harder when you are set on fast-function mode all day and the change of tempo to a quiet at-home evening may seem like time wasted.

Matt Stone accepts that running his businesses means being away from home a good deal but he keeps in mind, always, that he wants and needs time for family.

'It is a huge help if you can be very organised and make realistic plans for work in a manageable way. Using digital tools is also very helpful as is a bit of common sense. These days I put my foot down at long meetings or people wanting to take up time when they are not focused on what needs discussing or doing. The other thing is I have learned to say "no" to are things that I know will overload me or take time I have planned for my private life.'

His determination is focused by having two teenage children and a second marriage with a wife and young child:

'I very much want time with them. It helps that my wife and I are a good team around the home and I schedule in a date night weekly with my wife so we can have a bit of fun and a chance to talk properly about what is going on in our lives. We have just taken a longish holiday because I realise I haven't had a proper holiday in ten years, and my wife said it was time!'

Alex Norton describes his passion as *Malevolence,* the online game he has created, and is realistic enough to know that he does not want children who would require a radical change of his focus. As it is, he has time and energy for the love and strong connection that he describes with his wife Nyssa, as well as being able to devote the time he wants to his game, and neither would want to unbalance that. Alex explains:

'She is an avid gamer herself, which means she has been able to understand the importance of my project. She is like the guardian of the gates to my solitude - she will instantly recognise when I am focusing on something and will work to make sure I stay undisturbed. I am a bit of a sociopath when it comes to work and life balance but luckily my wife loves me for my passion and dedication to my craft.'

Yet he sees that it may be time to open up life so that it is less work-focused:

'We have seen only a small handful of friends in the early years of *Malevolence* which [tended to] fill the weekends, but in the last couple of years I have started making time to step back from things from time to time. I have reclaimed my weekends and gotten back into hobbies and am spending more time among people. And I draw inspiration for the incredibly detailed mathematical nature of my game, from nature - the great harmony of all things.

'I hike for miles into the wilderness to be away from noise and the bustle of life. My wife often joins me and it keeps us strongly connected. We've been through enough together that would have seen weaker relationships crumble, but for us it just made things stronger. That might have been much harder if we had not been able to have as much time as we do to shape as we wish.'

Homepreneurs

It is very encouraging to see environmental concern being flagged up by the guys who started *Enterprise Nation*, a resource for people starting and growing a business at home in the UK. Their forward thinking is significant for Lifestyle Entrepreneurs because they have brought a vital, but not always recognised, fact to our collective eyes and ears. In 2007, they launched a Savings Calculator to demonstrate savings in time, money, and carbon emissions, that can be made by working at home. They found that home-based workers save on average £4,392 in travel costs, 564 hours commuting time, and 2937 carbon emissions per year.

That is one aspect of their work, but they also demonstrate that working from home has many advantages for a healthily balanced and co-operative family life. The Workhome authors discuss how important it is for LEs to be able to combine paid employment with their caring responsibilities. To illustrate this they offered examples of people living the Workhome life, ranging from the MD of a manufacturing company who had set up his business so he could help his partner with their severely disabled child, a hairdresser who had started a home-based salon when she became a single parent, to an alternative health practitioner who cared for her elderly mother in an adjacent flat.

So it made me very cross indeed to hear how the UK government is 'slow to recognise the potential of this working practice nationally', while over in the US they value 'hompreneurs' who generate £303 billion a year.

Even if you are in the workplace as an employee, many people are seeing how possible it would be to 'graduate' to being home-based altogether. Sociologist Catherine Hakim found that almost without exception every occupation - and the list covers academics and architects to canine beauticians, CEOs of third sector organisations, funeral directors, mechanics, wedding chauffeurs and a great many others - had homeworkers.

Between 1991 and 2010 it was estimated that a quarter of the working population of the UK lives at their workplace or works at home for a minimum of eight hours a week. Does this situation suggest that being in the workplace full-time, or indeed at all, is actually necessary for people to be able to work successfully?

Keep the office door shut

Because she has children living at home and needs a sense of a boundary between work and home life, Christine Fogg would not do as Suzanne Noble does, who keeps several income-generating balls in the air at once and works on the kitchen table. It's a way for her to be sure she can keep her focus on the varied, and often complicated, commitments she takes on.

'I have a room in the family house that is my office and the children know if I am in there with the door shut I am working, but I try to keep working hours to between nine in the morning and three in the afternoon when they are at school. And I try to make time with children a chance to see friends too. So for example I tend to have mothers and their children for tea on Fridays. I also make a point of booking out holidays well in advance, so my clients know, otherwise it can be difficult to take them.'

Give family life space

Jane Hamnett, 43, editor and proofreader, believes you need to be careful about letting work eat up family time if you work from home. Because there is not the formality of completing a work day in employment, it is all too easy to let work overflow into time allotted for bath-time with children, a welcome-home drink with a partner, enjoying making a meal in a leisurely way, having time to de-stress with feet up and a good book, or any of the other things that are the contrast between work and home life. She explains:

'My office is upstairs and it can be hard to switch off and stop working for the day [or] resist the temptation to go upstairs and check emails. But I have to be aware of this because sometimes I realise I don't have enough time to spend with my children.'

As a Lifestyle Entrepreneur, I often have to remind myself of how important work-life balance is with my partner and not get too absorbed into thinking I must make more money to be in the 'safe zone' financially. To combat those sorts of urges, I make sure we have specific uninterrupted times together every day or two so we can relax and enjoy each others' company.

Physical and psychological freedom

David Nicholson is very positive about working at home, although he makes sure he spends some time out socialising and networking. But he is also clear it would be a great deal harder if his wife were home too because it is the sense of aloneness he cherishes and which he believes enables absolute concentration.

'I have a sympathetic spouse and it is good that she has a conventional job outside the home. I have tried having offices away from the house, but I have an extra room now and that is economical in cost and time. So a better way.'

There is a common belief that working from home and for yourself will almost certainly mean earning less than in an employed job provided it has an honourable wage policy, although increasingly, even if the pay is okay, there is often little long-term security. Even people who, in the past, would have had jobs for life, are now likely to have time-limited contracts.

In fact, Meral Karamuk came from her native Turkey to Britain with her husband and has succeeded in creating a multi-stream income generating life with children's stories, theatre plays and articles. She also translates different types of text from English into her native language and does some proof reading.

She says 'I am highly motivated and enjoy challenging work. I am writing for children because I love their world and endless imagination.'

Most importantly she adds, 'My son and my family life are more important than my job and my career. So I am planning my working hours according to my son, my husband and our cat Tabitha. Mostly I work while my son is at school or after he goes to bed. I try not to work weekends.

'I wouldn't want a full-time job away from home because I don't want to leave my son with a childminder. I want to spend my own time for him, for my husband, for my other family members and for our home. If I had a full-time job I wouldn't be able to do this.'

And she is clear the family gains in a way they would not if she worked away. 'My husband is happy that I am home with our son and the boy learns how to work from home with discipline and of course with fun because that is what he learns from me. Sometimes he sits by my side and watches me work. He asks loads of questions and offers me help to finish my work early so we can play football in the garden together.

'I can work from anywhere if I have an Internet connection and notebook. I don't need a car to go to work, I can take a break any time, any week, any month or year. I love the way of work like this. I feel free and I can work at anytime, anywhere, even in any country so even if I could work less hours and earn more in a job I wouldn't consider it.'

Lucy McCarraher, who runs *Re-Think Publishing* and does a number of related writing and editing jobs, is clear about what she gives and gets:

'I work more and at a higher quality than if I worked for a boss. I am not motivated by working for someone else - or someone else's requirements. I like working for authors (publishing, editing) and for delegates (in workshops) - but on the occasions I have worked for others, or in offices, I have found myself unintentionally working to rule.

'Nowadays work mostly expands to fill the time around my family. Which is fine, because I'm almost exclusively doing things I love to do. I can go out and shop or have lunch when I want, but I don't do it much. I'm extremely disciplined, but it's not a conscious thing anymore, I've internalised the length of time it takes me to do anything, how much time I need to leave before a deadline, and so on.

'Occasionally, at my most insecure (financially), I have thought, 'Why did I never pursue a real career, get a proper job, sort out a pension...?' But I know the answer - I would have hated it. I always start a new activity thinking this is going to be the one that really makes me some money...Eternal optimism, being a risk-taker and loving new challenges has taken me on this journey, and I am very clear that I have enough to live on which is good enough.'

The financial cost of her choice is greater for Helena Appio, who works long hours, usually earns modestly, and makes sacrifices in her social life because of this. But it is a bargain she has made with herself and believes, in company with other multi-stream earners, that the ever interesting, engaging, stimulating life she has is a choice she stands by. She considers what she can spend on her social life:

'It is very important to understand that the day must include all the work that needs doing to meet orders or deadlines and that means all the hours it takes. You are in charge and carry the can, so it's what must be done.

'I certainly work harder than if I had a job with set working hours and workers' conditions. I am 57 and I have been working for myself for 12 years but I still haven't achieved an income comparable to when I was on staff at the BBC.

'I love working at very different jobs and the idea that if I have a new passion I can try to make it an earning stream. I resigned from the BBC because of the constraints and I am so much happier even though it means not going to expensive restaurants, or holding very smart dinner parties. I don't spend much on clothes or gadgets. I don't smoke or drink - all of which is fine because it means I can afford my freedom. It is a bargain with myself and I don't live in a hovel or starve, my income allows for a bit of travel and fun. The bottom line is that I drop everything if a job comes up and needs doing.'

Minimise external distractions

If you work at home, you need to learn to field interruptions that eat up time and disrupt your train of thought. Perhaps answering the door to a delivery is a must, but stopping to have coffee with a neighbour who calls unexpectedly is not. A polite 'so sorry, too busy just now, but can we fix a later date' is an effective way of dealing with such situations. Likewise, be clear that personal phone calls do not work for you during your working hours but that you would love to hear from them at an allotted time.

Increasingly, people who have work that demands clear focus and not losing their train of thought turn off their emails after they have checked and dealt with them first thing, then do it again at, say, lunchtime, and at the end of the day. Some people find it best to save answering any but the most imperative until the evening.

Obviously, it can be tricky to go incommunicado if you have clients who are likely to want immediate attention, or if a job comes in that you need to respond to instantly. If this is the case, you need to be very firm with yourself about only dealing with the most imperative communications as they arrive. Most things can actually wait as they would have in the past, before we all became so compelled by instant contact.

It is important if you work at home, when things so easily overlap, to try being strict about keeping mobile phones, iPads, computers and so on away from intimate family times like meals, watching a film, reading books and playing games together. Nothing breaks the closeness with friends and family like the command of a phone ringing and then a conversation about work suddenly intruding. Or if you quickly check emails and then react in a way that destroys the mood. Even a quick glimpse at a funny item you suddenly remember hearing about on YouTube can be very disruptive unless it is something you share and enjoy with whoever is around.

There has been plenty of research showing how badly it impacts on children if we get home from the office and carry on what we were doing there with our phones, tablets and so on. So is it any different if we allow this technology we may have been using all day to dominate time allotted to private life? There is a story that sticks with me, of a small girl whose mother spent a great deal of time on her mobile phone. No matter what she was doing with her child, if the phone rang, she dropped everything and often got into long chats. Her daughter tried sulking, crying, trying to attract attention while her mother was talking, but nothing worked. Finally she took a large bite of her mother's ankle and - bingo - her mother dropped the phone and rounded on the child. At least she got attention at last.

And it isn't rocket science to see how relationships are frustrated and put under strain if one partner is constantly engrossed elsewhere. It may be essential sometimes to be available for a business call as we have discussed, but it is worth doing everything possible to have an 'untouchable' time of the day when clients know your phone and computer will be turned off.

Sick days and holidays

One thing about working from home and for yourself is that nobody will pay you for a sickie, or a few days off when you have vile flu and really cannot work, let alone if you get a more serious, long-term illness. So it is very important to calculate into your budget a margin of money to deal with this, and other happenings that cost money at a time you cannot earn it. It may be worth looking for an inexpensive insurance that will pay for when you are ill or have an accident as self-employed people do not get sick time off.

Another important point is that you will need to think about saving from, say, the beginning of the year for a summer holiday. If you have no fallback position, it can be very stressful and potentially difficult financially, for your family. It can be hard, if you are having a fallow patch, to limit what you spend in order to feed this kitty, but it is well worth making it a must-do. In fact, I do this myself by trying to save a minimum of £100-200 per month so I can treat my wife to a nice holiday together someplace and always buy the flights / pay for the holiday well in advance.

As a very popular member of People per Hour, Marina Mercer knows it can be hugely helpful to use 'automatic' salesmen who will make sure you don't miss a client while you are out. For example, set an out of office reply, add a widget for linking to your site, and make sure your profiles make plain when you are selling services or not. Or there are organisations that offer a telephone answering service, where a real human being, not a disembodied robotic voice, attends to the person calling. But of course this is an added cost so you have to weigh up whether it will pay.

Another way of helping yourself through a seemingly impossible pile up of work may be to employ someone on an ad hoc basis from one of the online services offering skills that can be bought per one-off job. For example, for this book, we had a People per Hour provider transcribe taped interviews and do some research for us. Or there may be a student with skills useful to you who would be happy to do a couple of weeks if they have free time. Alternatively, among the unemployed there may well be people who would be delighted to help out temporarily.

Create a balance

The idea of a good work-life balance has got into the collective psyche in the past decade, as more and more people recognise the high price of giving too many of our most vigorous hours to the workplace while nearest and dearest and friends get the scrag-end of our time and zest. But it may be harder to recognise that you are doing this if you work at home because we somehow assume that being physically present, even if locked away in an office, is good enough.

It is not. The integrated life means paying careful attention to balancing needs and nurturing relationships and situations in our life on a par with what we give to our work. That said, there will be times as I described above when the pull is against balance, and it is not useful to beat ourselves up and indulge in spirit-sapping guilt. The point is to keep ever in mind our ideal and to try to compensate for an imbalance.

But there will also be times like this last weekend, when I worked more dynamically than I had anticipated, got through what appeared an impossible mound of tasks related to several different income streams, and freed myself up to have a longer stretch of time to go off to a friend's wedding with my wife, relaxed and high-spirited knowing I can take two days off for rest and relaxation before I gear up for the next round of tasks. If I had an employed job and worked especially hard I wouldn't be rewarded with an extra chunk of time off - just be patted on the back by a satisfied boss at best.

12

WHAT SUCCESS LOOKS LIKE

What we see in this book is an approach to work that outs the emphasis on entrepreneurialism and multi-stream earning, it is a new approach to work with the potential to be quite radical in offering a sustainable alternative to signing up for the workplace and working for a boss. It suggests an answer to the dilemmas of what work is, whether it is available at all, who has the control over how we do it, how we are treated, and who gets the profits from our labours, which is one of today's big talking points.

We also see how the Lifestyle Entrepreneur way helps us achieve a constructive integrated life at a time when relationships from the very young all the way up to the over 60s are often splitting apart. Divorce is at a higher rate than ever, and that is often blamed on the pressures of working life, too little time for the personal and too little of the sharing and caring time we all need.

But at the heart of this is the all-important question: do those who have chosen the Lifestyle Entrepreneur way see theirs as success stories? Are they living lives that have worked out, or are working out as they wish? And what does success mean to them? Here, some of the people we have talked to along the way describe what success looks like to them.

It is striking how few people we came across - and this is true of all generations who have chosen the LE way - who are motivated simply by making a great deal of money, although some as we know do become wealthy or even mega rich, but that has rarely been their main drive. There is a powerful sense that feeling good with who and what LEs are in the world matters.

Sophie Amoruso, as you may recall, was enough of a success to publish her memoir at the age of 30, by which time she had amassed millions of dollars with her business Nasty Gal. But success is not about a stroke of luck, or a face and body that became iconic enough to pull in vast sums. She dissociates herself from too many people who she sees as clinging to the idea of entitlement. That is not the way this erstwhile, bottom-of-the pile young woman turned her life around so dramatically, and she says severely, 'a lot of people in my generation don't seem to get that you have to work your way up.'

So for those prepared to buy into the extreme work ethic she has, and which led to her creating several income streams from her original idea, along with a lifestyle that allows her to remain a stylish maverick, and making much of it on social media, she is an encouraging LE icon.

In 2015 she resigned as CEO of Nasty Gal, by then a $100 million fashion empire. She has gone on to establish the GIRLBOSS Foundation, which awards a $15,000 grant to women in design, fashion, music and the arts on a biannual basis. So far the foundation has been granted over $70,000 in funding.

Sophie says to give your idea your all but keep it true to who you are, and you can almost see a finger being wagged as she says, 'don't you dare alter your inner freak.' Which seems to be what success looks like to Sophie.

No office or boss for me

One of the things I have learnt researching and writing this book is how many others feel similarly to me about life looking and feeling very different, in a good way, when you dive into the LE lifestyle. A sense of freedom, even if you are working extremely hard is one of the things that Lifestyle Entrepreneurs voice, over and over, as a very definite measure of contentment.

David Nicholson has been a LE since he left university and is very clear about the things that make his life a successful one, even though he has had lean times, self-doubting times, and times of being over-stretched. As we have seen, he loves his work, enjoys the freedom from having a boss and answering to any corporate employer, and takes plenty of holidays to exotic places while staying in luxurious hotels.

Matt Harris has built up good earnings from the music he makes and sells online and, although he acknowledges that 'the money is great', the thing that really lights him up is being able to earn a decent living doing something he loves and have the freedom to shape life as he wants it at the same time. He is, in many ways, the definition of a successful sustainable entrepreneur:

'Freedom. That is the biggest thing. The ability to be the master of your own destiny and having that control over how much you earn because you're in the driver's seat. Psychological freedom, physical freedom, to me it's a huge benefit. It's not necessarily something you get when working for somebody else and you don't have an itinerary set for you during the day.'

He adds cheerfully, 'Because of the way I work, I'm pretty much unemployable and I've proved to myself time and time again that I can't work for somebody else. Their ideals rarely fit in with my own because I have my own way of approaching things and unfortunately that doesn't make me a particularly strong team player. This is what it's all about, the fact that I'm in control, and being a bit of a control freak, I'm just more suited to that way of working.'

While Helena Appio, who may have as many as six earning streams at any one time, is in no doubt about what she values as a Lifestyle Entrepreneur:

'It will be my life I think. I know I can earn money somehow, so I am not frightened. It is a psychological mindset you have to achieve. I consider I have a very interesting life. I love to try things and have the time to do so. I left the BBC to have freedom.'

Another measure of feeling that you have led your working life in the right direction is being able to use your creativity the way you think best. Besides the years spent exploring her entrepreneurial prowess by thinking laterally as well as logically, acting on impulses and dealing with clients the way she wants, Suzanne Noble can now take her creativity in an entirely new direction as the decision maker.

Within months Suzanne was celebrating how well her company Frugl was doing with an excited missive to supporters:

'It's an exciting time for the business. We launched on iOS last year, have amassed thousands of downloads and a very loyal, active user base. By the end of the summer we will have a full suite of products across mobile platforms (iOS and Android) as well as the web putting our real-time marketplace in a very strong position for future growth.

'Frugl is very excited to have been chosen by Google UK as one of just ten businesses to enter their pilot programme for 'Founders over Fifty' that launched recently. Frugl can look forward to a large amount of publicity and attention as a result of this association as Google will be putting all their marketing and PR weight behind it.'

There is a momentary pause as she sums up: 'I have a life I thoroughly enjoy and how many people on the work treadmill at my age can say that? I am focused on Frugl, my entertainment app, in a big way at present, but I still have interesting other projects in publishing and my charity work. I work from home, organise my time as I wish and have plenty of friends living similarly to socialise and network among. Is that success? It is to me.'

There may be bad times ahead

If you're not failing every now and again, it's a sign you're not doing anything very innovative - that at least is how Woody Allen sees it. He could be speaking straight to Lifestyle Entrepreneurs, for whom the essence of success is so often being innovative and bold.

You may work insane hours, meet deadlines, get gratitude from clients, but still hit a bad time. It could be that you miscalculate the possibilities of an enterprise; key people you have working for you jump ship; one of your markets goes bust. Or you could behave in a way that does harm. Football coach Gerard Jones, who we met earlier, has made a good deal of money in his early 20s and admits he didn't cope well with sudden fame:

'I had my downfall, I learned about being naive, my behaviour wasn't what it should have been, my business slipped down to a level that did worry me, so that was a lesson. But there was nobody to blame but myself, so I had to just find a way to get back up by working very hard to re-build my reputation and by focusing on being a decent person. And now I'm doing OK. I am lucky to be in demand and I earn well. I don't need to be Mickey the Millionaire. That's not what I'm about.'

Nor did Sophi Tranchell have the smooth trajectory her early time with Divine Chocolate suggests. She talks of how 'the financial crisis gave us an absolute kicking.' and in 2008 and 2009 the business was badly hit by the global financial crisis. Divine was hit by the falling value of the pound and higher cocoa and milk prices, and the UK's supermarkets cut back on how much space they gave to luxury chocolate brands, recognising that fewer people would be able to afford them.

With *Divine Chocolate's* profit margins badly hit, Sophi says she had no choice but to cut back on its promotional work, which meant it lost ground against its competitors. Impressively, she managed not to have to cut any jobs among 15 UK staff. 'It really strangled our growth,' she says. But a continued drive and effort has paid off and the company is now growing again, by 8% per year, and while it makes annual UK sales of £8m in a market worth £3.9bn, it remains a tiny company, Sophi agrees, but has interesting times ahead as it merges its UK and US businesses making a bigger, stronger and more resilient foundation on which to grow.

On the other hand, it is demonstration of how the entrepreneurial spirit can make a success of something improbable and she has declared, 'I do hope that Divine will inspire people to think that their dream is possible, because it was so unfeasible that we would make a success of it.'

No less, given how important fighting for humanitarian values are to Sophi, she describes herself as 'still a radical,' and Divine Chocolate is a Fairtrade venture that is 44% owned by a collective of cocoa farmers who get their percentage of the profits and have two seats on the board of the company. Sophi puts the reason for her satisfaction with the way of work she has chosen this way: 'I have always been interested in who is controlling what…and I'm very keen that people don't feel hopeless. If we all do something we can make a difference.'

Suzanne Noble who, as we have seen, is doing well with Frugl nevertheless tells of the tough 'moment' she has been having trying to raise funding for expansion of her app:

'I've found fundraising to be extremely stressful and challenging. I don't think anyone can fully comprehend how much effort and time is involved until you do it. This is the first time I've felt the need to raise money as all my other businesses have grown organically. But running a tech business with a view to becoming a global business isn't the same as running a niche PR agency in the UK; it takes deep pockets. The accelerator I was on certainly gave me a good grounding in creating a business plan but, since then, I've learned an enormous amount. If I'm honest, that period of time seems like a very long time ago!'

Onwards and upwards

I've had my fair share of 'failings' when starting my income streams. Things like, in the early days, writing entirely the wrong type of music for the marketplaces I sell on, pitching music for adverts that I would now consider poor and unfinished, approaching directors and producers in a brash and brazen manner (which is not conducive to getting work from them!), and even presenting myself online via my website in a way I now know was completely unprofessional.

But this is part of becoming an LE, you must learn to adapt, recognise where you went wrong and keep going as you will inevitably learn from your mistakes and experimentation.

A matter of balance

As a writer of novels and complementary health books and teaching, Pam Ferguson, who is twice my age and could teach me a thing or two about multi-stream earning, having done it for decades, believes creating balance is an important part of feeling good with the LE way:

'Select jobs that complement each other or at least offer enough variety to keep you ever interested and alert. For example I found it hard when I lived in London to be a journalist and work in public relations at the same time - too close. I don't have that conflict with being a writer and a teacher as both are independent careers and I have carved a global niche in both.'

The sense of living the right life that comes from balance is very clearly at the heart of how Lucy McCarraher has run her LE life, although she focuses the thought differently:

'You really need to love what you do ideally…if we are talking about success I certainly see this as a measure of what I have been able to achieve - having a life that I love and that has been shaped to fit the way I want to live and at the same time having a life where I can offer opportunities to other people. Success is about how you view the world, how you feel about yourself, because that is much of what you are selling, what comes across to clients.

'So I would say that having a self image which includes seeing yourself as creative or entrepreneurial and enjoying rather than fearing risk-taking is a significant part of it. You need to believe everything is going to work out somehow. I see myself as an eternal optimist. I am driven by always believing this is the new activity that is going to be the one... will take me places and make me some money. The pleasure of multi-stream earning is that there is always the possibility.'

Matt Stone who, you may recollect, left the car dealership he worked with for several decades when he realised they were not treating him with the recognition and respect he felt he deserved for the work, and success, he brought to their company, is a relative newcomer to the LE world. But his positivism surely tells of how gratifying it can be to be brave enough to make a big shift at a time when many are counting the years until their pensions kick in. It was, he says, an epiphany of sorts.

He realised he did not want to return to corporate life, but thought - correctly - that he could use his various business skills to set up his own enterprises. And he gets much satisfaction from giving time mentoring.

Changing his way of working and living has also been an important way of moving life on, he says, after a 'nasty divorce which was a hideous experience, but I like to think I turned being financially at rock bottom, and feeling I had little to lose, into a positive. I was able to see an opportunity and say here I am in my late 30s, I have always wanted to scratch the itch I had through years of being employed, to test my abilities my way and evolve new skills, and I feel that is what has happened. That to me looks like success.'

None of the three involved in launching the *Wild Card Brewery* doubts the risk they took in following their collective dream was the right thing, so it is very pleasing to hear how well things are going. Andrew Birkby updated me with an outburst of excited enthusiasm:

'Things are going very well indeed. We've doubled the capacity of the brewery and are looking to increase it again this summer. This we have done using peer-to-peer lending from local supporters. We are getting on board with bigger and bigger customers. And we recently exported beer for the first time to France.

'The bar at the brewery is also going from strength to strength. It is also starting to develop a good reputation as a music venue. We have had gigs ranging from local London bands launching their albums at an early stage in their career to world renowned musicians such as Javier Zalba of Buena Vista Social Club and

Thurston Moore of Sonic Youth.'

So yes, he feels he can talk of success and offer a measure of it:

'For us success is about getting enough healthy income streams coming into the business that we're free to focus on what we enjoy: making great beer. For example it is terrific being able to invite customers into our brewery bar to have a drink with us and bring them closer to the product. But it also gives our business another leg to stand on by providing additional income streams and that secures us more freedom to experiment in the brewery.

'It feels like we're well over the initial hump. We owe a lot to our local community who helped and supported us in getting there because, we think, they like that we have taken a risk to pursue something we are passionate about.'

Respect as success

Alex Norton says, 'I've always said that I'd rather die a poor, but respected man than die a rich man with no respect, and while I may not be able to derive a full-time pay cheque from my game-making as yet, it has earned me a huge amount of respect from my lovely community and also my peers. I am regularly called upon to give talks and advice as an expert in my field, I am well respected by many in the games industry and above all I have the admiration and love of a small but dedicated community who understand me as a person and not just as a game developer - who can see my passion and get involved in it themselves.

'Having reached that stage in my career at my young age and with only my first commercially released game is quite an achievement, and covers many steps on my road to what I would consider to be true success for myself. One day I'll reach the end of that road, but until then, it's winning the little things like that which make a huge difference in the scheme of it all.'

Emma-Jayne Parkes and Viviane Jaeger, at six years into their business, are still relative newcomers to what being entrepreneurs means and although *SquidLondon* is in a 'growth phase' as they add

SquidKids childrenswear to their brand, and are launching in Hamleys in the Autumn of 2014, there is no question of relaxing although a little mutual back-patting is allowed.

Emma-Jayne spells out how success feels at this stage: 'it is very much based on demand. The popularity of the product and the excitement it creates when we explain it to people is still a driving force. It is an honour to be contacted by the head buyer of *Cirque de Soleil* asking if we could design them a bespoke item to sell. We started *SquidLondon* in our final year at University because we wanted to see our product on the market and so we are pleased with what we have achieved so far. And mums, bloggers, children, buyers have all said how much they love it. But we have no illusions: there is an even bigger journey ahead. On the other hand we feel more equipped than we did six years ago and positive we will make it work - one way or another!'

So in these pages we have heard from people of different backgrounds, qualifications, philosophies, and ages, all who have chosen to create lives as multi-stream earners. We see a groundswell of creative and innovative thinking, a determination from a growing number of people that they must generate their own solution to the work-life balance as well as making work pleasure, not pain. So it is that we see projects like SquidLondon, SocialSpider, Nasty Gal, and the many others written about here, growing from the inventive imaginations of people who want to design their own work, and to shape their lives to fit the way they want to live.

The new millennium Lifestyle Entrepreneurs are creating a way of living and working that is good for the soul as much as the bank balance, representing a real and sustainable re-shaping of what work means in our lives. It echoes the thinking of Bob Dylan: 'What's money? A man is a success if he gets up in the morning and goes to bed at night and in between does what he wants to do.'

13

THE 5-STEP PLAN

If you've reached this far in the book, you're probably interested in trying the Lifestyle Entrepreneur approach for yourself, so we've put together a brief summary of the main points in this book for becoming a multi-stream earner. While this is not an extensive in-depth guide to everything required, it will serve as a starting point from which you can build your own ideas, check you've got the fundamentals covered, and begin exploring how to profit from your passions.

1. Pinpoint your passions and skills
Start by writing down absolutely *everything* that you consider your passions, skills and interests. As mentioned, I like to create Mind Maps as they show all my ideas laid out in a nice and clear manner (also see the earlier mind map in chapter for reference):

Now you have all your potential earning avenues laid out in front of you, it's time to choose 2-3 areas you're particularly passionate about - these should be your primary interests from all the ideas you've pieced together. Don't worry if you're not 100% sure you'll love doing these things forever, the beauty of the LE approach is that you can change direction later or refine your decisions if you find you're not as passionate about something as you originally thought - remember, you're your own boss!

Brainstorm ideas in a list (or create another Mind Map!) around how you could potentially profit from each of your 2-3 ideas you've chosen. You'll want to make sure you can make enough to survive on from each of these ideas before you proceed. Now break down your sections into niche areas if possible, to see if you can identify a specific area of the industry you're particularly interested in, yet has low competition.

I find it helps to define the *purpose* of ideas, i.e. why are you choosing this idea? Are you going to do this work for more money? More freedom? To give something back to your community or maybe gain respect within your industry? Identifying the core reason behind your ideas will give you an important focus as you develop your income stream further.

Ask yourself whether you'll be making best use of your skills with your idea, or whether you'll need to outsource a lot to get your idea going (this might need an investment). Finally, evaluate how much time you have to dedicate to each of these ideas now, where you want to go with it in the future, and decide which is your strongest idea to try. By forming an idea of where you want to get to, you'll have a better focus and plan to reach your goals (which can change later of course, depending on what is and isn't working).

2. Evaluate the landscape

So, you've identified a strong idea and have a good idea of where you want to go with it. Is there a market for it? Check the places where your target audience is and see if anything is selling, whether online or offline. For online income stream ideas, check places like People per Hour, Fiverr, and Upwork to see if there's any interest or movement in the market you're targeting.

If a bunch of people are earning money there (check reviews, sales, recent work submissions they've made), and particularly if you think you could produce something better than what they're offering, whether now or in the near future, then there is likely a market for your product or service. You should also conduct some research offline, even if it's as simple as asking friends, families and strangers if they would be interested in X or Y or find it useful. If their eyes light up, you could be onto something.

What are you going to charge, and how does it compare to the competition? What will you need to realistically charge in order to survive and cover your costs? Identify your *baseline rate* and make sure you aren't running into ruin with guns blazing.

Make sure you research who your competition is (if any) and look at what they're charging, where they're marketing, who their providers are (if any) and how they're dominating the market. I put a Mind Map together for each competitor with branches and look at whether it's worth competing with them directly, or whether I should go more niche to avoid working against companies with big marketing budgets.

Lastly, a useful technique for testing the interest of a particular niche online is to use Google's Keyword Planner tool to investigate what people are searching for, and identify the best long tail keywords for your online campaigns. By knowing this information, you can see whether people are searching for what you're offering already.

3. Prepare

After evaluating the landscape, you should consider putting together a business plan, even if it's basic, so you have a roadmap for how your business/ income stream will progress. For tips on how to write a business plan, see here: gov.uk/write-business-plan. Do you have a name for your business and some basic branding?

How will you find sources of work? Will you start on an online marketplace if your product / service is digital, or go solo straight away with your own (paid or free) website? If your product or service is physical, will you sell at a market or business expo that is open to the public? Will you cold-call or deliver leaflets locally to get new leads? Try writing down some ideas of where and to whom you will pitch your ideas (this can come in handy later as well when you're stuck on what to do during quiet periods).

Create a structure to your day and put together a work checklist if it helps you focus on the tasks at hand and to stay productive. This includes how you will approach things like social media and other marketing materials. Remember to see how much time you have available for each part of your plan, and structure things so that your days are manageable.

Are you primarily trying to earn a passive or active income? If you're aiming for a passive income, bear in mind that income can come slowly and in small amounts, particularly in the beginning. Consider your physical location: how and where are you going to start operating? If it's at home, make sure you have an area free of distractions (and temptations). Setting up next to the TV with a couple of packs of chocolate at arm's reach is probably going to be harder to get going in rather than a nice quiet room.

Consider your costs - will you have any software or machinery requirements? Note down how much each costs if so, and for how long you will need it so you can weigh up how you can recoup those costs later through your earnings, or through funding. For example, are there renewal, subscription or rental costs? Will the machinery wear away quickly and need replacing often? Remember the important motto, 'earn more than you spend'. Do you need funding to get going? Would crowdfunding be a viable source of funding for your project?

Do you need to do some training, or improve your skills or product, before you approach your market? Sometimes you'll want to just get yourself out there quickly like I did, but if you'd feel more comfortable doing some preliminary training, then start by looking for free tools and courses online (even if it's just YouTube tutorials) or invest in a paid course or two if you have the budget. Always ask whether it will help set you apart from the competition and bring you a return on your investment later on.

Finally, where are you going to keep the money that comes in and how will you record your expenses? Do you need an invoicing and project management system like thrivesolo.com, freshbooks.com or basecamp.com? Are you clear about how much you need to earn to cover your taxes and any legal costs etc.? And don't forget to register as a self-employed individual or a company if you're going down that route. Tax affairs are an important step, so don't skip it!

4. Release and test, test, test

Here comes the fun part. You've done all the hard work of preparing your income stream, got your ducks in a straight line, and now it's time to tweak things to find what works best. By this point you'll have a good idea of whether there is interest in what you want to earn from and will have done arguably the most arduous part of becoming a Lifestyle Entrepreneur: the preparation.

Some people like to create some pre-buzz and do a 'soft-launch' of their product or service. This consists of telling people a specific amount of time before you actually launch (usually a month or two, but some people even do it up to a year in advance) that you're going to release something pretty exciting into the world. Many businesses create 'countdown' websites using a service like getresponse.com, unbounce.com or launchrock.com and send people to them via marketing materials. By collecting people's email addresses, you can contact a bunch of people who are *already interested* in your product / service just before you launch, on the same day and then follow up with an offer. It's a good way of kickstarting your income stream.

And remember that testing is a continuous process, so it is worth setting up a spreadsheet to monitor what works and what doesn't, so you can work smarter rather than harder and focus on techniques that are giving you a return. Don't forget that you will be one of millions of other people competing online, so get testing with different marketing techniques so people actually know about you - no one can buy from someone they don't know exists!

Test whether you're getting more business online or offline. Sometimes, it can be surprising how much work you can pick up offline, and locally, in comparison to focusing entirely online, particularly if you're offering something that local businesses or individuals will benefit from. Use all the tools at your disposal, from social media, printing out some leaflets if you're targeting locally, and putting posters in shops close by, to maybe paying a small amount for some advertising via Google or Facebook (make sure you've done your keyword research well to get the best results), advertising in a local paper, or even doing something unusual so you stand out, like creating an entertaining comic that subtly advertises you.

Lastly, don't forget to ask friends, family or a mentor for feedback on your ideas and what else you might test.

5. Reflect, review and plan for the future

While testing is an important step, so is reflecting on how you're going in relation to your vision that we established in step two. Look at the response of your efforts and reflect on how you could improve things - have you been pushing too hard with marketing techniques that your customer base doesn't relate to? Do you need to be more conversational and informal? Has the advertising brought in more customers or do you need to start looking for customers elsewhere?

Reflect and review often (I'd recommend once a month, even if it's just for an hour), as you'll be more successful in the long run if you do more of what works and tailor your efforts to your audience. Adapt and continue testing as you progress, and you'll recognise early on if you need to change your model.

If you're not having much success, keep positive (this happens to *everyone* in any business) and investigate why you're not getting any traction. Do you need to improve your offer? Up the quality of your product or service? Is it a particularly slow time of year (like summer holidays or Christmas)? Are you too expensive or too cheap in comparison to the competition, or is there no interest because you're marketing in the wrong place? There are usually reasons for a sluggish market.

Part of preparing for the future is questioning whether you can (or need) to bring in other people to help. It's often cited that many businesses receive 80% of their income from 20% of their clients

- do you have particular clients who are draining your resources, meaning you're neglecting the ones who are efficient, pay well, on time, or do business in a way you enjoy? If so, and you've reached a point where you could survive from fewer clients, trim the ones who are taking up more energy and time than is necessary and push on finding more of the good clients. You CAN fire bad clients and feel okay about it - business is a relationship between two parties.

It can be useful to build an online presence with a social media account, like a YouTube channel or Twitter profile, and stick to a plan of regularly building a subscriber count. The more you do this, the more potential leads you'll have in the future and a following you can build a relationship with. By cold-calling potential clients (whether yourself or hiring in someone to do it for you) you can also prepare yourself for the future. Remember to get their emails and learn about them a bit before contacting them.

If you're short on work, continually extend your reach through business directories, local events and driving traffic to your website via your social media account(s). Remember to start an emergency fund for your business for times in need, and never forget to top this up each time you earn.

You'll need to pay tax on any income and cover running costs (like transport, software and machinery), so make sure you have earned enough from your income stream to justify any outsourcing or investments you have in mind for the future. Try creating a content marketing plan for how you're going to double the interest in, and potentially your income from, what you're offering. Does that require buying advertising, producing regular content online, offering freebies, using tools like the mass email software MailChimp to reach out, or even just creating your own publicity materials like photocopying flyers to put in new places locally?

By looking ahead as well as reflecting on how your income stream is doing, you can keep your business healthy.

ACKNOWLEDGEMENTS

I'd like to give a special thanks to my clients and customers both past and current who have been great to work with, put their trust in me and allowed me the space to develop my work life in a way that works for me.

We owe great thanks to Cassie Weber for the impeccably researched, hugely detailed dossier she created for me as a very valuable starting point for this book. Elena Georgieva did some excellent interviewing and fact finding and it was a pleasure working with her. Lexy Hudson deserves big thanks for doing a very meticulous critique of the manuscript and making many valuable suggestions. The many and varied people I interviewed who so willingly gave their time, stories and at times guidance. They have added an enormous richness to this book.

We would also like to thank the following people for their help and contributions in making Lifestyle Entrepreneur possible and for being an inspiration to me: Tim Hulse, Suzanne Noble, David Nicholson, Sara Charles, Jonathan Self, Lynda Gratton, Andrew Scott, Michael Bihovsky, Matt Stone, Natalia Talkowska, Lucy McCarraher, Matt Harris, Jennifer Sheridan and Matthew Markham, Mark Playne, Molly Berry and Juan Bronson, Zek Hoeben, Kimiko Shiga, Isana Banana and little Seiji, Kimberley Pryor, Simon Ratcliffe, William Harris, Andrew Birkby, Jaega Wise, Helena Appio, Viviane Jaeger and Emma-Jayne Parkes, Sophi Tranchell, Barbara Gunnell, Jonny Mundey, Martin Bright, Alex Norton, Miriam Lahage, Andrew Denham, Katharine Hibbert, Emily Perkin, Becky John, Professor Nicos Nicolaou, Ian Merricks, Neeta Patel, Michael Young, Paul Nicol, Mark Esho, Mark Pearson, Ed Molyneux, Barbara Gunnell and Jonny Mundey, Alex Feldman, Kate Cook and Bruce Goodison, Elaine Pofeldt, Pamela Ferguson, Gérard Jones, Christine Fogg, Rameet Chawla, Sophie Amoruso, John Greathouse, David Floyd, Mark Brown, Jason Jones, Trent Hamm, Alyson Shontell, Nicko Williamson, Jamal Edwards, Martina Mercer, Jane Hamnett and Meral Karamuk.

I (Angela) am indebted to my delightful daughter in law Carolina Diaz Rosado for allowing me to dominate chunks of Cato's time which he could otherwise have spent with her. But I hope she thinks the result worth it. And of course I want to thank Cato for being a highly professional co-author - even though there were a few early moments when I thought working together would end in a toss up between matricide and infanticide.

RESOURCES

Starting a business
UK GOV advice
(gov.uk/browse/business/setting-up)
Writing a business plan (gov.uk/write-
business-plan)
US government advice
(irs.gov/Businesses/Small-Businesses-&-
Self-Employed/Starting-a-Business)

Business ideas
forbes.com/sites/danschawbel/2012/05
/31/how-to-start-a-business-with-only-
100-in-the-bank/
theselfemployed.com/start_ups/50-self-
employed-business-ideas-can-start-100

Crowdfunding
crowdfunder.co.uk
crowdsourcing.org
crowdsunite.com
moola-hoop.com
nesta.org.uk/blog/crowdfunding-skills-
challenge
*UK regulatory regime for crowdfunding
platforms finalised*
out-law.com/articles/2014/march/uk-
regulatory-regime-for-crowdfunding-
platforms-finalised/
E-book on crowdfunding
weblaw.co.uk/ebooks/crowdfunding-
guide.pdf

Platforms for selling your digital product(s)
digitalgoodsstore.com
intubus.com
sellfy.com
gumroad.com
fetchapp.com

payloadz.com
pulleyapp.com
simplegoods.com
sendowl.com
selz.com
getdpd.com
e-junkie.com
plasso.co
trychec.com
fastspring.com

Loan options
startuploans.co.uk
UK Government Finance and support
for your business
gov.uk/business-finance-support-finder
betterbusinessfinance.co.uk
virginstartup.org

Marketing websites

General
ducttapemarketing.com/blog
entrepreneur.com)
michaelhyatt.com)
Content creation
copyblogger.com)
kaushik.net)
contently.com/strategist/
boostblogtraffic.com
contentmarketinginstitute.com
copyhackers.com
thesaleslion.com
thecopybot.com
marketingprofs.com

SEO (search engine optimization)
moz.com/blog

searchenginewatch.com/seo
searchenginejournal.com
distilled.net/blog/
searchengineland.com
seobook.com/blog

Online Marketing
blog.kissmetrics.com
johnfdoherty.com
unmarketing.com
unbounce.com/blog
quicksprout.com/blog
hubspot.com
chrisducker.com/blog
digitalmarketer.com
usertesting.com/blog
blog.crazyegg.com
sproutsocial.com/insights

Advertising and social media
ppchero.com
socialmediaexaminer.com
blog.bufferapp.com
jeffbullas.com
socialtriggers.com/blog/
socialfresh.com
swayy.co
writtent.com/blog

Sites on which to sell or hire services
fiverr.com
peopleperhour.com
odesk.com
voicebunny.com
freelancer.com
3to30.com
guru.com
elance.com
taskrabbit.com
99designs.com

Domain registrars
ukreg.com
123-reg.co.uk
godaddy.com

Cheap web hosting
hostgator.com
asmallorange.com
dreamhost.com
bluehost.com
liquidweb.com
1and1.com
unitedhosting.co.uk
swbroadband.co.uk

Medium cost web hosting
hosting - wpengine.com
pagely.com
mediatemple.net
rackspace.com

All-in-one website services
squarespace.com
weebly.com
wix.com
virb.com
strikingly.com
tumblr.com
Wordpress.com

Landing page/ launch website services
getresponse.com
unbounce.com
launchrock.com
templates only
themeforest.net/category/ marketing/
unbounce-landing-pages

Invoicing / Project Management software
thrivesolo.com
freshbooks.com
zoho.com/invoice
basecamp.com
zoho.com/projects
salesforce.com
sugarcrm.com
paymoapp.com